The Cycle of Day and Night

Samantabhadra

Namkhai Norbu

The Cycle of Day and Night

where one proceeds along the path of the primordial yoga

An Essential Tibetan Text on the Practice of Dzogchen

TRANSLATED, EDITED AND INTRODUCED BY
John Myrdhin Reynolds

Barrytown
Station Hill

Second Edition, revised and expanded. The first edition was published under the auspices of the Dzogchen Community in America (Conway, Massachusetts) by Zhang Zhung Editions, Berkeley, California, 1984.

Published by Barrytown/Station Hill Press, Inc., Barrytown, New York, 12507.
Email: publishers@stationhill.org
On-line catalogue: www.stationhill.org

Produced by The Institute for Publishing Arts, Inc., a not-for-profit, tax-exempt organization in Barrytown, New York.

The publisher gratefully acknowledges permission to use the following illustrations:

The cover, depicting the Dzogchen Master Garab Dorje, a detail from a painting by Nigel Wellings, now in the collection of John Shane, © 1987 by John Shane; the frontispiece by Gomchen Oleshay, © 1984, 1987 by Gomchen Oleshay; and all other illustrations in the book by Nigel Wellings, © 1984, 1987 by Nigel Wellings; the back cover photograph of Namkhai Norbu by Susan Quasha.

Cover design by Susan Quasha.

Library of Congress Cataloging-in-publication Data

Norbu, Namkhai.
The cycle of day and night.

Bibliography: p.
1. Rdzogs-chen (Ruin-ma-pa) I. Reynolds. John Myrdin.
II. Title
BQ7662.4.N68 1987 294-3'444 87-9953

ISBN 0-88268-040-4

Printed in the United States of America

Contents

Vajrasattva

Preface

This text, entitled in Tibetan *gDod-ma'i rnal-'byor gyi lam khyer nyin mtshan 'khor-lo-ma,* was written by Namkhai Norbu Rinpoche prior to a retreat led by him at the Dzogchen Community of Conway, Massachusetts, in October, 1983. In the *Longde* Series of Dzogchen teachings, there are found the instructions of Garab Dorje on how to practice contemplation continuously both day and night.[1] The present text is a synopsis of these practices.

According to the Buddhist tradition of Tibet, Garab Dorje was the first human teacher of the Dzogchen system of contemplation practice. The Tibetan term Dzogchen has usually been translated as "The Great Perfection" and in Tibet it represents the quintessence of the Buddhist teachings. Garab Dorje is said to have been born in the country of Uḍḍiyāna to the northwest of India and to have received the transmission of Dzogchen immediately from Vajrasattva, the *sambhogakāya* aspect of Buddhahood. Vajrasattva had received the transmission directly in a mind-to-mind fashion from the Primordial Buddha Samantabhadra. From Garab Dorje, Dzogchen was transmitted to Mañjuśrīmitra, and from him to Buddhajñāna and Śrīsiṃha. In the eighth century C.E., the transmission of the Dzogchen precepts was brought to Tibet by Guru Padmasambhava, Vimalamitra, and the translator Vairocana.

From the time of the above masters, the Dzogchen teachings have been transmitted from master to student in an uninterrupted fashion. In the system of the Nyingmapa sect of Tibet, Dzogchen, which is also called Atiyoga, is known as the ninth vehicle among the nine vehicles into which the teachings of the Buddha were classified. However, the introduction of Dzogchen into Tibet long antedates the rise of sects among Tibetan Buddhists. Many eminent masters belonging to the four principal sects of Tibetan Buddhism, including such illustrious figures as the Fifth Dalai Lama, the Third Karmapa, and Drugpa Padma Karpo have practiced these teachings openly. Many others have practiced them secretly. Therefore, it is certain that Dzogchen is not the exclusive property of any one sect and, in truth, these teachings transcend any sectarian, cultural, or national limitations.

Dzogchen pertains to understanding in one's immediate experience the primordial state of the individual, the unconditioned nature of the mind. This nature of the mind transcends the specific contents of mind, the thoughts arising in the mind which reflect one's psychological, cultural and social conditioning. One may make the same distinction between the mirror which has the natural and inherent capacity to reflect and the reflections which are seen in it. The mirror is not to be confused with the reflections which appear in it. The presentation of Dzogchen here, shorn of such limitations, follows in the Rimed or non-sectarian tradition of the recent great masters of eastern Tibet, such as Jamyang Khyentse Wangpo, Jamgon Kongtrul, Chogyur Lingpa, and Adzom Drugpa.

The numbers found in the translation of the text refer to the individual verses in the Tibetan text. The notes which follow the translation are arranged accordingly. These notes are drawn from the oral commentary to the text given by Namkhai Norbu Rinpoche at the Conway retreat, October 8-9, 1983. At that time, Norbu Rinpoche spoke in Italian, while Kennard Lipman and John Shane translated the commentary into English.

Finally, the translator of the text wishes to thank Dr. Kennard Lipman and Mr. John Shane for their invaluable assistance in rendering this text into proper English. He also wishes to thank the many members of the Dzogchen Community of Conway who participated in this project in one way or another. May this translation prove of practical benefit to all who read it.

SARVA MANGALAM.

John Myrdhin Reynolds
Conway, Massachusetts
November 1983

Preface to the Second Edition

The edition presented here is substantially the same as the first edition published in 1984 (Zhang Zhung Editions, Berkeley, California)—although the translator has done a considerable amount of editing of the notes, which are in the form of a continuous commentary to the translation of the Tibetan text. These notes were originally taken from the oral explanations of Namkhai Norbu and edited by the translator. In this second edition there is also a newly written introduction. The translator wishes to thank Mr. George Quasha of Station Hill Press for offering the opportunity to bring out this new edition. He also wishes to thank the members of the Dzogchen Community of Conway, who originally sponsored this translation, for their help and encouragement, and especially Nina Robinson for all her inspiration, patience, and encouragement.

J.M.R.
Conway, Massachusetts
July 1986

Introduction

The text which we have translated here, the *gDod-ma'i rnal-'byor gyi lam-khyer nyin mtshan 'khor-lo-ma,* or "The Cycle of Day and Night, where one proceeds along the Path of the Primordial Yoga," by Namkhai Norbu Rinpoche, is not an academic introduction to Dzogchen; it is neither a treatise on the philosophy of Dzogchen nor a scholarly survey of the extant Dzogchen literature in Tibetan. Rather, it is an upadeśa,[1] a teaching on the essential points of Dzogchen practice. It explains with great precision, in detail although concisely, how to practice contemplation continuously during the day and the night. Traditionally, an upadeśa is a secret oral instruction given in private by a master to his disciples who are committed to the path to realization. Such an upadeśa is drawn from the personal experience of an accomplished master, who has himself attained a definitive degree of realization in the practice, where he touches upon certain essential points, both theoretical and practical, which are directly relevant to the practice and experience of the yogin.

Namkhai Norbu Rinpoche is such an accomplished master. Born of a noble family in Derge in eastern Tibet, he received the finest academic education available, which, in the case of Derge, was that of the Sakyapa school of Tibetan Buddhism.[2] In addition, he was early recognized to be a reincarnate Lama or *tulku*—in this case, the tulku of Adzom Dugpa (1842-1924), who was one of the most famous masters and teachers of Dzogchen in eastern Tibet at the turn of the century. Later, he was recognized by the sixteenth Gyalwa Karmapa and Palpung Tai Situ Rinpoche to be the reincarnation of the illustrious Dugpa Pema Karpo (1527-1592), the leading master and scholar of the Dugpa Kagyudpa school of Tibetan Buddhism. But the essence of Dzogchen is not found in academic scholarship nor does it require the credentials of ecclesiastical hierarchy. Dzogchen is beyond all such intellectual and cultural limitations. It was not until he met his own root Guru (rtsa-ba'i bla-ma)[3] that he came to understand what Dzogchen meant in terms of direct personal experience and realization. The master in question was Nyala Changchub Dorje (1826-1978), a Nyingmapa Lama and physician who was the spiritual leader and guide of a community of lay practitioners in a remote valley in eastern Derge. From this master, Norbu Rinpoche received the most important transmissions of the three series of Dzogchen teachings: the Semde, the Longde, and the Mangagide.[4] (For further details concerning the life of Norbu Rinpoche, see the Biographical Sketch of the Author in this volume.)

It was out of his own personal experience and personal realization of Dzogchen that this text was written. But here there is also a melding of tradition with the personal experience of the master. In the Longde (klong-sde) series of Dzogchen teaching, there are found instructions on how to practice contemplation continuously both day and night. In particular, there is the *Byang-chub sems bcos thabs mdor bsdus*[5] by Garab Dorje, who, according to the Buddhist tradition of Tibet, was the first human teacher of Dzogchen on our planet. The present text by Namkhai Norbu Rinpoche gives a synopsis of these practices. Since Dzogchen in general, although now it is considered to be a part of Tibetan Buddhism, is not well known as yet in the West, it will be necessary here to say a few things concerning its place in Tibetan Buddhism and something concerning its origins.

In Tibet, Dzogchen has traditionally been regarded as the highest and quintessential teaching of the Buddha. It has usually been associated with the Nyingmapas, the oldest school of Tibetan Buddhism, although Dzogchen in itself is beyond any such sectarian limitations. Moreover, the introduction of Dzogchen into Tibet long antedates the rise of religious sects among the Tibetan Buddhists. These sects only came into existence with the renewal of translation activity from Sanskrit into Tibetan in the eleventh century C.E. Although Dzogchen has frequently been linked to the Nyingmapa school, due to that school's role in being the custodian of traditions deriving from the Old Translation period (7-9 cen. C.E.), Dzogchen is in fact not a sect or a school of philosophy. Rather, it is a path to the realization of our primordial state which is beyond conditioned existence, and as such, it is not limited by any particular cultural or historical context.

The Tibetan term Dzogchen (rdzogs-pa chen-po) corresponds to the Sanskrit Mahāsandhi, and is usually translated as "the Great Perfection." This teaching is called the Great Perfection because it is complete and perfect (rdzogs-pa) in itself, there being nothing lacking in it, and because it is great (chen-po) in the sense that there is nothing greater than it or beyond it. But, fundamentally, the name Dzogchen refers not to a philosophical teaching among other philosophical teachings, but to the primordial state of the individual, our inherent Buddha-nature, which is synonymous with the nature of the mind. In the Dzogchen Tantras, especially those of the Semde (sems-sde) series,[6] this primordial state is known as the Bodhichitta, and in this context the term has a different meaning than it does in the much better known Sūtra system of Mahāyāna Buddhism. In the Mahāyāna Sūtras, the Bodhicitta, "the thought of enlightenment," is the resolute intention of the Bodhisattva to attain the supreme enlightenment of a Buddha for the sake of benefiting and liberating all sentient beings from Samsāra, the beginningless cycle of death and rebirth. But in the Dzogchen Tantras, Bodhicitta has a very special meaning.

The Sanskrit word Bodhicitta in its Tibetan translation, *byang-chub sems,* is interpreted in Dzogchen to mean *byang* "pure" from the very beginning (ka-dag); *chub* "perfected," that is, spontaneously self-perfected (lhun-grub); and *sems* "mind" signifying the unobstructed energy of compassion. Primordial purity (ka-dag) and spontaneous perfection (lhun-grub) are the two aspects of the primordial state of the individual; in the nature of the mind they are inseparably united (dbyer-med). The aspects of the primordial state may be tabulated as follows in terms of their implications:

Essence (ngo-bo)	emptiness (stong-pa nyid)	primordially pure (ka-dag)	Dharmakāya (chos-sku)
Nature (rang-bzhin)	luminous clarity (gsal-ba)	spontaneously perfected (lhun-grub)	Sambhogakāya (long-sku)
Energy (thugs-rje)	unobstructedness (ma 'gag-pa)	inseparably united (dbyer-med)	Nirmānakāya (sprul-sku)

The primordial state is a unity, but in order to speak of it and its manifestation, we distinguish these three aspects (chos gsum). The Essence of the mind, which is primordially pure, is emptiness and this is the Dharmakāya. Its Nature is luminous clarity, which is spontaneously self-perfected, and this is the Sambhogakāya. Its Energy is unobstructed and all-pervading and this is the Nirmānakāya. The primordial state is the nature of the mind and this manifests as its Essence, its Nature, and its Energy.

Every spiritual path may be analyzed in terms of its Foundation (gzhi), its Path (lam), and its Fruit ('bras-bu). In the case of the Hetuyāna or Causal Vehicle, which is the system of the Mahāyāna Sūtras, the Foundation or Base is our inherent Buddha-nature, the Path is the practice of the six perfections of generosity, morality, patience, vigor, meditation, and wisdom by the Bodhisattva over the course of three immeasurable cycles of time, and the Fruit is attaining the Trikāya, the three dimensions of the existence of a Buddha.[7] We speak of a causal vehicle here because there exists a cause, our inherent Buddha-nature. But this Buddha-nature is only something potential, like the seed of a great tree planted in the earth. Many secondary conditions, such as season, rain, and so on, are required to bring it into germination, maturation, and fruition. In the same way, the accumulation of merit and the accumulation of wisdom is required to bring our inherent Buddha-nature into fruition as the manifestation of the Trikāya.

However, in the case of Dzogchen, the view is quite different. The Trikāya is already fully manifest as the nature of the mind from the very beginning, although it has gone unrecognized due to accumulated layers of emotional and intellectual obscurations —just as the face of the sun in the sky may be obscured by clouds. Although invisible to us, nonetheless, the sun is present there in the sky all the time, so that when the clouds dissipate, the sun becomes clearly visible. It is the same with Buddhahood; it has been there all the time, although we have not recognized it. Although unrecognized, the Trikāya is already, from the very beginning, fully manifest as the Essence, Nature, and Energy of the mind. Thus we can say of Dzogchen that the Foundation is the Trikāya, the Path is the Trikāya, and the Fruit is the Trikāya. Dzogchen represents the Phalayāna or Fruitional Vehicle, that is to say, the effect is already present as the cause.

In Dzogchen, a clear and crucial distinction is made between the nature of the mind (sems nyid) and the mind (sems), that is, our thought processes, the incessant flow of discursive thoughts (rnam-rtog) which continuously arise within us. We must clearly understand the difference here if we are to understand Dzogchen. There is a traditional metaphor to help us comprehend this. The nature of the mind is like a highly polished mirror, whereas the individual thoughts, emotions, impulses, feelings, sensations, etc., which arise are like the reflections in this mirror. The Tibetan word *rig-pa,* which we can translate as intrinsic awareness or pure presence, is similar to the capacity of the mirror to reflect whatever is set before it, whether beautiful or ugly. The opposite of *rig-pa,* "awareness or presence," is *ma rig-pa,* "ignorance" or the absence of awareness. With presence and awareness we live in the condition of the mirror, so to speak, whereas with ignorance we live in the condition of the reflections, thinking that whatever appears before us is substantial and real. With intrinsic awareness we exist in the condition of Buddhahood, while from ignorance we find ourselves entering again into the cycle of transmigration. When we speak of the primordial state (ye gzhi), we mean the nature of the mind (sems nyid) in the state of being just as it is (ji bzhin nyid), which is beyond time and conditioned existence. Buddhahood is already fully realized and manifest from the very beginning as the nature of the mind, although up until now it has gone unrecognized.

The function of the Guru or master (bla-ma) is to introduce (ngo-sprod) us to the nature of the mind, to its capacity for presence and awareness (rig-pa). Entering into this state of intrinsic awareness is what is meant by contemplation (ting-nge 'dzin, Skt. samādhi). Contemplation must be clearly distinguished from meditation (sgom-pa). Intrinsic awareness is beyond and outside of conditioned existence and the temporal process; it is beyond the mind, whereas meditation involves the working of the mind. It is, therefore, conditioned and occurs in time. The master first introduces us by indicating in our immediate experience what is mind and what is the nature of the mind. There exist many methods to help us realize this distinction concretely and these are known as Khorde Rushan ('khor 'das ru-shan), that is to say, discriminating between Samsāra ('khor) and Nirvāna ('das). Here Samsāra means mind (sems) and Nirvāna means the nature of the mind (sems nyid). These Rushans constitute the actual Ngondro (sngon 'gro) or preliminary practices for Dzogchen. What Western students usually know as the Ngondro is not Dzogchen, but the preliminary practices for Tantra, the path of transformation.[8] Nonetheless, all of these Sūtric and Tantric practices can be profitably used by Dzogchen. But what is absolutely essential is Guru Yoga (bla-ma'i rnal-'byor), for Dzogchen, like other spiritual teachings, is dependent upon transmission, and the Guru Yoga is the principal means for maintaining all of the transmissions that one has received.

The earliest sources for the Dzogchen teachings are the texts known as the Dzogchen Tantras. These were originally set down in writing in the language of the country of Uddiyāna, which is akin to Sanskrit. In ancient times Uddiyāna was a country to the northwest of India.[9] In general, the teachings of the Buddha are found in two classes of discourses known as the Sūtras and the Tantras. All of these teachings have been regarded by the Tibetan Lamas as Buddhavacana, the authentic word of the Buddha. The Buddha taught many different kinds of doctrines and practices, not because He was inconsistent or did not know the truth, but because the capacities of His listeners differed in terms of what *they* could understand. So as an expression of His great compassion and His skillfulness in means He taught each disciple according to the latter's level of comprehension, in order that he might understand and be able to practice the teachings. All of these teachings are classified according to the three vehicles to enlightenment, namely, the Hīnayāna, the Mahāyāna, and the Vajrayāna.

The Nyingmapa school of Tibet has more precisely classified these teachings of the Buddha into nine successive vehicles (theg-pa rim dgu). The first vehicle is that of the Śrāvakas, "the listeners" or Hīnayāna disciples. This path was principally indicated in the first discourse of the Buddha which He gave at the Deer Park of Sarnath near Varanasi and is known as "the First Turning of the Wheel of the Dharma." In this discourse He expounded the Four Holy Truths and the Noble Eightfold Path. These teachings are thoroughly elaborated in the Hīnayāna Sūtras. The second vehicle is that of the Pratyekabuddhas, the silent Buddhas or those who attain realization in solitude. The Śrāvakas are "listeners" because they need to hear the oral instructions of the Buddha in order to find the correct path, whereas the Pratyekabuddha finds the path on his own and then lives a life of solitary meditation practice in the wilderness, avoiding all communication and contact with humanity. For this reason, he is compared to a rhinoceros, an animal known for his solitary and antisocial habits. These two vehicles together comprise the Hīnayāna or lesser vehicle to enlightenment, and it is so called because its goal is only the personal salvation of the individual practitioner, to the neglect of others. The principal method employed here is the path of renunciation (spong lam). In the case of the Hīnayāna, the Foundation is disgust with the world, the Path is the threefold training in morality, meditation, and wisdom, and the Fruit is the personal liberation from Samsāra of an Arhat (in the case of the Śrāvakas) or of a Pratyekabuddha.

The third vehicle is that of the Bodhisattva. A Bodhisattva is an individual who is on his or her way to becoming a fully enlightened Buddha and thus the Bodhisattva by-passes the lesser goal of the Arhat. A Bodhisattva becomes one by virtue of producing the Bodhicitta, "the thought of enlightenment," or the resolute intention to attain the enlightenment of a supremely perfect Buddha, not just for his own benefit, but for the sake of rescuing and liberating all sentient beings from Samsāra. This path is known as the Mahāyāna, "the greater vehicle," because its goal is correspondingly greater—a universal salvation, the liberating from Saṃsāra of all living beings and not just oneself alone. These teachings are found in the Mahāyāna Sūtras, which contain the discourses given by the Buddha at the Vulture Peak near Rajgir and elsewhere. These discourses represent the Second and Third Turnings of the Wheel of the Dharma, wherein the Buddha expounded the Perfection of Wisdom (prajñāpāramitā) and the Mind-only (cittamātra) teachings respectively. Out of these two sets of discourses there later developed the two philosophical schools known as the Mādhyamaka, which taught the middle way that avoids all extreme views, and the Yogācāra which principally taught the mind-only doctrine. In the case of the Mahāyāna, the Foundation is one's inherent Buddha-nature, the Path is the practice of the six perfections by means of which one accumulates merit and wisdom, and the Fruit is the realization of Buddhahood. The principal method employed here is the path of purification (sbyong lam). The teachings of the

Hīnayāna and the Mahāyāna are collectively known as the Sūtra system and are said to have been revealed by the historical Buddha, Śākyamuni, who is the Nirmānakāya aspect of Buddhahood.

The outer or lower Tantras comprise the next three vehicles of this scheme of classification. The methods delineated in these Tantras employ elaborate rituals and purifications. The principal means here, as was the case with the Mahāyāna Sūtras, is the path of purification, and for the Yoga Tantra also, in part, the path of transformation. The fourth vehicle is that of the Kriyā Tantra, where the practice is mainly external, requiring a considerable amount of ritual activity. Hence its name, for *kriyā* means ritual action. The fifth vehicle is that of the Caryā Tantra, which is partly external and partly internal in terms of practice. There are many rules for conduct here; hence its name, for *caryā* means conduct. The description found in the Kriyā and Caryā Tantras of how Buddhahood is attained is the same as the account found in the Mahāyāna Sūtras. The sixth vehicle is that of the Yoga Tantra, where the practice is mostly internal, that is to say, visualization rather than ritual, and the actual union (yoga) of the practitioner with the meditation deity is experienced. The teachings found in the Tantras are said to have been revealed by Vajrasattva, the trans-historical Saṃbhogakāya aspect of Buddhahood. Collectively, the teachings of the Tantras, both outer and inner, are known as the Vajrayāna, "the diamond-like vehicle" to enlightenment. They are also known, in contrast to the Sūtra system, as the Tantra system.[10]

The inner or higher Tantras comprise the three highest vehicles of the Mahāyoga, the Anuyoga, and the Atiyoga. The seventh vehicle, the Mahāyoga, which is subdivided into the Tantra section and the Sādhana section, employs elaborate visualizations of deities and mandalas, putting the emphasis on the Generation Process (bskyed-rim) or stages of creation. This represents a process of gradual transformation, so that the visualization of the deity and of the mandala is created or generated in successive stages. The method of the higher Tantras is properly that of the path of transformation (sgyur lam). A traditional metaphor illustrates this. A Hīnayāna practitioner comes along the road and seeing the poisonous plant of the passions before him, he is afraid and avoids it because he knows the consequences of that poison. Then a Mahāyāna practitioner comes along the same road and seeing that same poisonous plant, he is not afraid of the plant touching him because he knows the antidote to that poison. He knows how to purify the poison by dissolving it in his meditation into emptiness, so that it will have no effect. Finally a practitioner of the Vajrayāna comes along the road and seeing the poisonous plant before him, he does not fear or hesitate to eat the fruit of that plant because he knows how to transform its poison into pure ambrosia. The method employed here is the alchemical transmutation of the poison of the passions within the vessel of one's own body into the elixir of enlightened awareness (ye-shes). This process in the Mahāyoga culminates in the realization of the experience of the inseparability of appearance and emptiness (snang stong zung-'jug). The newer schools of Tibetan Buddhism: the Sakyapa, the Kagyudpa, and the Gelugpa, relying upon the later translations of Indian Tantric texts, speak of the Anuttara Tantras, and these are said to correspond, more or less, to the older classification of the Mahāyoga Tantras.

The eighth vehicle, the Anuyoga, puts the emphasis on the Perfection Process (rdzogs-rim) or stages of completion. This process makes extensive use of the yoga of the channels and energies (rtsa-rlung) and it brings the practitioner to the experience of the inseparability of bliss and emptiness (bde stong zung 'jug). Here the method of transformation differs from that of Mahāyoga in that it may be gradual or non-gradual. In the case of these higher Tantras, the Foundation is the human body with its psychic channels and chakras, the Path is the Generation Process and the Perfection Process, and the Fruit is the realization of the Trikāya.

The ninth and highest vehicle, the Atiyoga, is also known as Dzogchen, a word which means, as we have said before, "the

Great Perfection." Here in Dzogchen, the Generation Process and the Perfection Process, that is, the elaborate visualizations of deities and mandalas, as well as the internal esoteric yoga of the channels and energies, and so on, are no longer necessary. The definitive method here in Dzogchen is not that of renunciation or purification or transformation as it is with the Sūtras and Tantras, but the path of self-liberation (rang grol lam). The emphasis is put on how to directly enter into a state of contemplation without any antecedent practice of transformation. The ensuing realization is the experience of the inseparability of awareness and emptiness (rig stong zung 'jug). The Dzogchen Tantras which are found in this class of Atiyoga belong to three series of teachings. First there is the Semde (sems sde) or "Mind series" which provides a rather intellectual approach, a step by step explanation of how to enter into the state of contemplation. It is rather similar to the Mahamudrā system of the Anuttara Tantras and is likewise divided into four yogas or stages. The Longde (klong sde) or "Space series" is more direct in its approach; the stages occur simultaneously rather than sequentially as they do in the Mind series. Finally there is the Upadeśa (man-ngag gi sde) or "Secret Instruction series" which assumes that one already knows how to enter into contemplation and so it gives advice on and methods for continuing in the state of contemplation. All of these teachings which are found in the Dzogchen Tantras are said to have been revealed by the Primordial Buddha Samantabhadra, the Dharmakāya aspect of Buddhahood, which in itself transcends conception by the finite intellect.

The Dzogchen Tantras are not directly attributed to the historical Buddha, Śākyamuni, who appeared and taught in northern India some two thousand five hundred years ago. However, Buddhahood, the principle of enlightenment, is not limited to some specific point in time and history. It is not as if Buddhahood was attained once and for all on some particular date and all we can do now is preserve the traditions of what happened then. Our salvation is not contingent upon faith in an historical event. Rather, Buddhahood is something which lies outside of history and the temporal process altogether; in a word, it is "primordial." But Buddhahood is equally ever-present in the hearts of all sentient beings as their potential for the realization of liberation and enlightenment. There exist no sentient beings who are not potentially Buddhas. However, even though it is ever-present here and now, during the course of a beginningless series of lifetimes, it has become clouded over by emotional and intellectual obscurations. But this Buddhahood is there all the time, just as the sun is always there in the sky, even though it is obscured by the clouds. When the clouds dissolve, the sun is clearly seen. In the same way, when our obscurations are dissolved, our inherent Buddha-nature, which up until that time has gone unrecognized, now manifests itself spontaneously, becoming visible in all its glory and splendour. The whole point of the spiritual path, and in Buddhist terms this means the practice of the Dharma, is to remove these dark layers of obscuration, so that our innate Buddhahood may shine through and illuminate our entire life and world.

Since the principle of enlightenment is beyond time and conditioned existence, Buddhahood can manifest at any time and is not restricted to a revelation or an incarnation that occurred only at one particular moment in time and history. It follows that the Dzogchen teachings were revealed and will be revealed many times over again during the history of humanity on this planet. In fact, the Dzogchen Tantras speak of the twelve great Teachers of Dzogchen who appeared in prehistoric times, Śākyamuni being the last in this series. Nor is Dzogchen restricted to the human race which now dominates this planet earth. The Dzogchen Tantras, and in particular the *Śabda-mahāprasaṇga Tantra,*[11] speaks of the thirteen star systems where Dzogchen is presently preserved and taught. Indeed, according to the same sources, only a small number of the sixty-four myriads of Dzogchen Tantras which exist are found extant in our world. Many of these Tantras are said to have been brought to this planet from other worlds and other dimensions of existence by human and non-human Vidyādharas. A Vidyādhara, or in Tibetan *rig-'dzin,* is an individual who has realized ('dzin) the knowledge of the primordial state (rig-pa).

When Buddhahood or the principle of enlightenment manifests on a plane outside of time and historical condition, this manifestation is called Vajrasattva. Such a manifestation has five supreme aspects (phun-tshogs lnga): The Supreme Teacher is the Saṃbhogakāya, Vajrasattva. The Supreme Place where He manifests is Akanistha, the highest plane of existence. The Supreme Retinue who is His audience is the great Bodhisattvas. The Supreme Doctrine is the highest teachings of the Mahāyana and the Vajrayāna. And the Supreme Time when this revelation occurs is eternity, which is outside the temporal process. When a Bodhisattva sufficiently purifies his mind and vision, then the realm of the Sambhogakāya comes into view and he can receive the teachings directly from the Buddha Vajrasattva. And so it came about that in many different regions of India, and elsewhere in Uddiyāna, after the time of Śākyamuni, there appeared certain great adepts or Mahāsiddhas, such as Saraha, Nāgārjuna, Kambalapa, King Jah, and so on, who received the revelations of the Tantras in this manner.

In the Dzogchen tradition, we speak of three principal types of transmission: 1. direct transmission (dgongs brgyud) which occurs in an instant, directly mind to mind, without any words intervening; 2. symbolic transmission (brda brgyud) through the visible display of signs and symbols, in silence or with only a few words; and 3. oral transmission (snyan brgyud) through explanation in words from the mouth of the master to the ear of the disciple. According to our tradition here, the ultimate source of the Dzogchen teachings is the Dharmakāya, the Primordial Buddha Samantabhadra (kun tu bzang-po), who is conventionally depicted in Tibetan scroll paintings as a naked azure blue yogin sitting in meditation position suspended in the middle of the sky. Although the Dharmakāya in itself transcends conception by the intellect and is inexpressible in words, we symbolically represent what is actually omnipresent and formless by this form in order to give our finite human minds some concrete sense of its profound and vast meaning. Samantabhadra is naked because the nature of the mind in itself is denuded of all discursive thoughts and conceptions; and He is the color of the sky because the nature of the mind is empty, clear, and open like the sky. He is called the primordial or Ādibuddha because He is beyond time and conditioned existence, and has at no time been caught up in Samsāra. He possesses the two purities: He is intrinsically pure and is purified of all adventitious taints. The Sanskrit term Dharmakāya means the dimension (kāya) of all Reality (dharma). The communication of the Dzogchen teachings from the Dharmakāya Samantabhadra to the Sambhogakāya Vajrasattva represents a direct transmission (dgongs brgyud), and the usual format in a Dzogchen Tantra for the presentation of the teachings, as for example in the Kulayarāja Tantra,[12] is that of a dialogue between Samantabhadra and Vajrasattva, the former being the Teacher (ston-pa) and the latter the audience ('khor). However, as it is explained in these Tantras, in actual fact the Teacher and His audience are identical; they only appear symbolically as two separate and independent entities so that the teaching may be presented to human understanding in dialogue form.[13]

Vajrasattva signifies the Sambhogakāya aspect of Buddhahood. However, in its collective aspect, the Sambhogakāya is conventionally represented by the five Tathāgatas, usually known in the West by the name the five Dhyāni Buddhas.[14] These five are also represented as being the audience for Vajrasattva, in which case, as it was so before, the Teacher and the audience are identical in essence. Vajrasattva is depicted as being white (or sometimes blue) in color, holding in His hands the vajra or diamond sceptre and the bell which signify the two coefficients of enlightenment, Compassion and Wisdom, respectively. He is attired in all of the precious jewel ornaments and exquisite silks once worn in ancient times by Indian princes. These symbolize the richness and over-flowing abundance of the manifestation of the Sambhogakāya. This Sanskrit word literally means the dimension (kāya) of enjoyment (sambhoga) and is so called because the beatific vision and the numinous presence of the Sambhogakāya is enjoyed by the great Bodhisattvas who have ascended the seventh through the tenth stages in the spiritual development of the Bodhisattva.[15] The Sambhogakāya possesses the five supreme aspects we mentioned above. The communication of the Dzogchen teachings from the Sambhogakāya Vajrasattva, residing in eternity on the highest plane of existence, to various Nirmānakāyas appearing on various other planes of existence represents symbolic transmission (brda brgyud). Although there have occurred throughout the ages many such transmissions to Vidyādharas belonging to such non-human races as the Devas, the Nāgas, the Yakshas, and the Rākshasas, in human terms the principal transmission was from the Sambhogakāya Vajrasattva to the Nirmānakāya Prahevajra, otherwise known as Garab Dorje.[16] For this reason it is said that Garab Dorje was the first human teacher of Dzogchen and that he was actually an emanation or incarnation of Vajrasattva.

Garab Dorje or Prahevajra was born in the country of Uddiyāna, which was located somewhere to the northwest of India. According to some sources this event occurred 166 years after the Nirvāna of the historical Buddha in 881 B.C.[17] In those days in the country of Uddiyāna there existed a very large lake called Dhanakośa, "the treasury of riches," and on the shore of that lake there was a magnificent temple called Śankarakūta, which was surrounded by some sixteen hundred and eight smaller shrines. This country was ruled by king Uparāja and his queen Prabhāvatī. The royal couple had a daughter, the princess Sudharmā, who grew into a virtuous and beautiful young woman. Upon listening to the Dharma being taught by certain masters, she decided to renounce the worldly life and take the vows of a bhikshunī or mendicant nun. Together with her maid servant Sukhā, she retired to an island of golden sands in the middle of the Dhanakośa lake, and living in a humble grass hut, she meditated and practiced the Yoga Tantra.

In a dream the bhikshunī beheld an immaculate glorious white male figure who came to her from out of the sky and placed on the crown of her head a crystal vase marked with the five syllables OṂ ĀḤ HŪṂ SVĀHĀ.[18] After consecrating her thereby, he dissolved into a ray of light and entered into her body, whereupon she was able to see everything in the three worlds clearly. The next morning, the bhikshunī recounted her dream to her maid servant and soon they discovered that the young nun was pregnant. Because this bhikshunī Sudharmā was a virgin and had never known a man, she became very terrified, fearing that her father the king and, indeed, the entire kingdom would come to hear of her dishonored condition. After some months a son was born to her. But, although this child was actually a reincarnation of a Deva Vidyādhara who had previously received the Dzogchen teachings in the world of the Devas, his mother did not recognize him.

Frightened and ashamed, the bhikshunī cried out, "This fatherless boy can be nothing other than an evil spirit!," and she threw him into a pit filled with ashes outside of her hut. Although her maid servant had observed that the child was marked with certain auspicious signs and warned the bhikshunī that the child might well be the incarnation of some great Bodhisattva, the distraught young woman would hear none of this. Nevertheless, at that very moment, many wondrous sounds were heard and rainbow rays of light appeared everywhere. Three days later, a bit subdued and conscience-stricken, the bhikshunī came out of her hut and went to look at the infant in the ash pit. Miraculously the child was unharmed and healthy. Immediately she recognized that he was an emanation (sprul-pa) and so, bringing him back into her hut, she bathed him.

At that moment, a voice from the sky exclaimed, "O our Protector, Teacher, and Lord who clarifies the nature of things and who protects the world, be our powerful protector! O Vajra of the sky, we pray to you!" The Dākinīs praised this miraculous child born of a virgin and made offerings to him.[19] Immediately he spoke and he began to teach the Dākinīs. This first teaching given by this child of miracles was called "The Great Sky of Vajrasattva" (*rDo-rje sems-dpa' nam-mkha' che*).[20]

When this child reached the age of seven years, he insisted that his mother permit him to go to dispute with the learned Panditas regarding the meaning of the Dharma. Finally, one day, after his mother had relinquished her opposition, the young boy went boldly to the palace of king Uparāja, who was, on that occasion, entertaining as his guest some five hundred learned scholars. This upstart young boy stepped unhesitatingly before the entire assembly and challenged these Panditas to debate with him. When the debate began, he put forth his arguments from the viewpoint of the Fruit ('bras-bu) and soundly defeated all five hundred scholars who had taken the viewpoint of the Foundation (gzhi). After he had defeated them, he proceeded to instruct them in the Atiyoga, the truth of which he had fully realized before he was born. These elder and venerable Panditas were completely astonished by the vast knowledge and penetrating insight possessed by this precocious child who was barely seven years of age, and thus the entire assembly of scholars made their prostrations to him. They came to call him by the name Prajnābhāva, "he whose nature is wisdom."

Since the king was absolutely delighted with this miraculous and precocious young boy and experienced an extraordinary rapture in his presence, he gave him the name of Prahevajra, which in the Tibetan language is Garab Dorje (dGa'-rab rdo-rje), "the vajra of supreme delight." And because his mother, the princess and bhikshunī Sudharmā, at his birth had thrown him into the ash pit, he also became known as Vetalasukha (Ro-langs bde-ba), "the happy vampire" and as Vetalabhishmavarna (Ro-langs thal mdog), "the ash-colored vampire."

Without ever having studied a book, this young boy knew from memory all of the Sūtras and Tantras of the Buddha Śākyamuni, as well as countless myriads of verses of Dzogchen teachings. Shortly after his birth, Vajrasattva appeared to him and conferred upon him the initiation which bestows total awareness (rig-pa'i spyi blugs kyi dbang), and the child came to realize that primordial gnosis which is beyond training (mi slob-pa'i ye-shes). Thus in an instant he comprehended the real meaning of all of the Tantras perfectly.

Later Prahevajra journeyed to the north, into the wilderness of the mountain solitudes which were haunted by the Pretas and other spirits. Here, in the place where the sun rises, he remained for thirty-two years. During this time, Vajrasattva again appeared to him in a brilliant sphere of rainbow light and bestowed upon him the secret instructions for the sixty-four hundred thousand Tantras of Dzogchen. Vajrasattva granted His permission for Prahevajra to write down these oral Tantras (tshig gi rgyud). Then, while still a young boy, residing in the mountain fastness of a peak of the Malaya mountain, together with the assistance of three Dākinīs, he wrote down these Dzogchen Tantras. In a cave on this same mountain, he concealed these Tantras as hidden treasures and appointed the Dākinīs to be their custodians.

While he was living in the wilderness among the craggy peaks, the earth trembled seven times. A Brāhmana priest in one of the villages below accused him of causing these quakes by his magic in order to injure the teachings of the Brāhmanas. The local Tīrthika king[21] therefore accused him of committing this crime and even the local herdsmen believed this and began to search for him. When the king's men arrived at the mouth of his meditation cave, they heard a deep and powerful sound coming from its entrance, like the roar of an Asura deep within the earth.[22] Thereupon a young man in the guise of a naked yogin appeared before the crowd, amidst rainbow rays of light, and no one could lay their hands on him. By means of this apparition, the king and his entourage were completely subdued and came to be converted to the Dharma. In addition, Prahevajra manifested many miraculous powers, such as walking upon the waters of a swiftly-running river, walking unimpeded through rock cliffs and boulders, and so on. He appeared before multitudes of people enveloped in a rainbow sphere of light, inspiring them thereby with great faith and devotion.

Then, mounting upon a Garuda bird of great and miraculous power,[23] he flew southward over the high Himālayas and eastward over the broad Gangetic plains to the great stūpa located at the cremation ground of Śītavana (bsil-ba'i tshal), "the cool forest," which is near Vajrāsana.[24] There he gave initiation and teachings to numerous disciples, including the Ḍākinī Sūryaprabhā. And there in that terrifying and awe-inspiring cremation ground, he remained for many years surrounded by hosts of Ḍākinīs.

At that same time, there lived a great scholar who was born in a city in western India as the son of a Brāhmana priest. Because he had completely mastered the five sciences[25] and because of his unsurpassed knowledge of the sacred scriptures, he became known by the name of Manjuśrīmitra. One day he had a vision and in this the great Bodhisattva of wisdom, Manjuśrī, advised him prophetically, "O son of a noble family, if you genuinely desire to attain the fruit of Buddhahood in this very life time, you should go to the cremation ground of Śītavana." Following this advice, the Āchārya (or master) went to the east and coming to Śītavana, he met Prahevajra. The latter said to him, "The nature of the mind has been the Buddha from the very beginning. This mind has neither birth nor cessation, for it is like the sky. If the real meaning of the ultimate identity of all phenomena is realized, and if that understanding is maintained without any seeking elsewhere, that is true meditation." Manjuśrīmitra immediately understood the true significance of this teaching.

Manjuśrīmitra remained there at Śītavana for some seventy-five years and from his Guru he received the transmissions of the entire Dzogchen Atiyoga which had originally come from Vajrasattva Himself. At the end of this period, Prahevajra displayed many wondrous signs, and his body becoming the nature of light, he dissolved into the sky. These manifestations indicated that Prahevajra had realized the Rainbow Body of light ('ja' lus). Manjuśrīmitra was overcome with grief and despair and he fell to the ground in a swoon. When he regained his senses, he cried out in lamentation, "O alas alas! O vast expanse! If the lamp of our teacher has gone out, by whom will the darkness of the world be dispelled?"

Instantly, his teacher appeared above him in the sky within a mass of rainbow lights. With the sound of a thunderclap, a golden casket, the size of a thumb nail, descended from this light in the sky. In the air, the casket circumambulated Manjuśrīmitra three times, and then fell into the open palm of his right hand. The vision of his teacher then dissolved again into the sky. When he opened the casket, he found the last testament (zhal 'chems) of the master Prahevajra, written with ink of lapis lazuli on the surface of five precious substances. Merely by the seeing of this testament, Manjuśrīmitra attained a realization equal to that of Prahevajra. This last testament, which sums up the entire meaning of Dzogchen, is known as "The Three Phrases which strike the Essential Point" (*tshig gsum gnad brdeg*).[26]

Manjuśrīmitra then set about to edit and classify the Tantras which he had received from his master into three series of teachings. Those teachings which emphasized the natural condition of the mind (sems nyid gnas-lugs) he classified as Semde (sems sde), the Mind series; and here, of course, "mind" means the nature of the mind or Bodhichitta. Those teachings which emphasized freedom from any effort (rtsol bral) he classified as Longde (klong sde), the Space series. Finally, those teachings which emphasized the essential points (gnad) he classified as Upadeśa (man-ngag gi sde), the Secret Instruction series. He further divided the most extraordinary teachings of the Upadeśa, which are known as the Nying-thig (snying-thig) or "essence of the mind," into two classes: the oral transmission (snyan brgyud) and the explanatory Tantras (bshad rgyud). At that time, since there was no one who was yet ready to receive the teachings of this first section, the Āchārya hid the texts beneath a huge rock to the east of Vajrāsana. He then retired to the cremation ground of So-sa-ling (so-sa'i gling) to the west,[27] where he remained for a hundred and nine years in meditation, practicing esoteric conduct (gsang spyod) with the Dākinīs and giving them teachings.

It was at this time that Śrīsiṃha came from the city of Sokhyam in China and he, together with Buddhajnāna, became disciples of Manjuśrīmitra. Previously, while traveling westward on a camel toward the city of Ser-ling in China, Śrīsiṃha had beheld a vision in the sky of the Bodhisattva Avalokiteśvara, who advised him, saying "O son of a noble family, if you desire to attain the fruit, go to the place in India called So-sa-ling." Later, leaving the holy mountain of Wu Tai Shan in northern China, having by then acquired many siddhis or powers, he went like the wind to India and at the cremation ground of So-sa-ling he met the Ācārya Manjuśrīmitra and received teachings from him for twenty-five years. At the end of his life, Manjuśrīmitra vanished from the top of the stūpa in the middle of the cremation ground. Then suddenly he reappeared in the sky and placed a small bejewelled casket in the palm of Śrīsiṃha's hand. Inside this was his master's last testament called the *sGom nyams drug-pa,* "the six meditation experiences." Upon reading these, Śrīsiṃha immediately realized the same profound intelligence as that possessed by Manjuśrīmitra. Śrīsimha also recovered the texts which had been concealed near Vajrāsana by his master. The Āchārya Śrīsiṃha proceeded to divide these into four categories: outer, inner, secret and exceedingly secret (phyi nang gsang yang gsang). These teachings he bestowed upon his disciples Vimalamitra and Jñānasutra. Later the Ācārya returned to China and at the end of his life he similarly vanished as a Rainbow Body. Thus, all the early masters of the Dzogchen lineage attained the extraordinary Rainbow Body of light.[28]

Both Vimalamitra and Jñānasutra also went to China to receive from Śrīsiṃha the oral transmission lineage of Dzogchen which the latter bestowed upon them over the course of twelve years while residing in the cremation ground of Śītakara. Later the Tibetan king Tisong Detsan[29] invited Vimalamitra from India and after coming to Tibet, Vimalamitra remained at Samye monastery for thirteen years. In this way, the Upadeśa series came to be transmitted to the Tibetans, as well as a portion of the Semde series. When he departed from Tibet, the Ācārya Vimalamitra went to the sacred Wu Tai Shan mountain in China.

Before the coming of Vimalamitra to Tibet, in the reign of the same king, Vairocana of Pagor had been ordained as a monk at Samye by the abbot Śāntiraksita. In fact, he was a member of the company of the first seven Tibetans to be ordained as Buddhist monks.[30] He was then sent to India by the king in order to continue his studies. At Vajrāsana he obtained all of the root Tantras for the Semde and the Longde. Thus it came about that these two classes of texts were transmitted to the Tibetans largely by Vairocana. In Tibet, Vairocana had also been a disciple of Guru Padmasambhava. However, this master principally taught Dzogchen in the context of Anuyoga, rather than as an independent system.

During his sojourn in India, while wandering through the sandalwood forest near Dhanakośa, Vairocana met the Ācārya Śrīsiṃha. At that time Śrīsiṃha was staying in a nine storied tower (ke'u tshang) which had been erected miraculously. But before the yoginī who served the master would conduct the young Tibetan into the presence of Śrīsiṃha, he had to demonstrate his own psychic powers. Coming before the Ācārya, Vairocana requested to be instructed in the vehicle which is without effort (rtsol med kyi theg-pa). However, it was necessary for him to study these teachings secretly at night because the local king had forbidden the spread of the Dzogchen teachings. The king and his ministers were afraid that this doctrine, which is beyond cause and effect, would undermine their own authority, and that of the state in general, over the people. And so, at night Vairocana wrote out the eighteen instructions of the Mind series (man-ngag sems sde) with goat's milk as ink on white cloth, so that nothing would be visible to the king and his men. Among these texts was included the first Dzogchen text which Vairocana translated into Tibetan, the famous *Rig-pa'i khu-byug,* "the cuckoo's cry of awareness."[32] The translation of the root text is as follows:

"Even though the nature of diversity is nondual,
In terms of individual things, it is free of conceptual
elaborations (made by mind).

Even though there is no thought of what is called 'just as it is,'
These various appearances which are created are ultimately good (transcending relative good and evil).
Since everything is complete in itself, abandoning the illness of efforts,
One remains effortlessly with presence in the state of contemplation."

However, Vairocana was not satisfied with the eighteen Semde instructions alone, and so Śrīsiṃha gave him the initiations and instructions for the other Tantras of the Semde series, and then for the white, black, and varicolored sections (dkar nag khra gsum) of the Longde teachings. Subsequently, Vairocana attained perfection in all of these teachings. At the cremation ground of Dhumapītha (du-ba'i gnas), "the place of smoke," he had a vision of Garab Dorje (Prahevajra) who bestowed upon him the sixty-four hundred thousand teachings of Dzogchen. Then he returned to Tibet by means of the power of speed running (rkang mgyogs) and he spread among his disciples the teachings of Dzogchen Semde and Longde.

The text that we have translated here opens with a salutation (mchod brjod) by the author to the masters of his own lineage of transmission. This is only proper because all spiritual teachings are linked with transmission. Then the author speaks briefly of the preliminary practices (sngon 'gro). With regard to the four meditations which bring about a change in our attitude toward life, the principal point is to be aware of their real meaning, rather than the performing of some elaborate intellectual analysis. The Tibetan term *shes-rig* conveys the meaning of being both present and knowledgeable, that is, we are aware of something we should know. For example, we should be aware at all times of the unique opportunity which this human existence offers us and that this life is impermanent. This awareness will motivate us so that we do not waste this present life in being distracted. But most important among all of these preliminary practices is Guru Yoga. The Guru Yoga (bla-ma'i rnal-'byor) is the most potent means to maintain all of the transmissions which we have received.

The principal section (dngos-gzhi) consists of a practice of the day (nyin-mo'i rnal-'byor) and a practice of the night (mtshan-mo'i rnal-'byor). In terms of the practice of the day, there are three topics to be considered. The first of these is understanding (rtogs-pa) the practice. In Dzogchen, the view (lta-ba) is regarded as even more important than meditation practice. Our view is the way we see and look at things, and "understanding" means not just an intellectual knowledge, such as we might get from a book or the classroom, but an entering experientially into a knowledge of the view. For this it is necessary to have the introduction (ngo-sprod) by the master in order to have indicated to us just what is presence or intrinsic awareness (rig-pa). If we do not have a concrete experience of this sort, then we will be dependent upon the descriptions which others give us and we can easily go wrong in our practice.

The second topic is stabilizing (brtan-pa) the practice. Once we have come to an understanding of the state of contemplation, of what is the real meaning of *rig-pa* in our own personal experience, next we must train in finding ourselves in this state of presence. Here there are three essential instructions (man-ngag gsum) to be considered. The first two, integrating (bsre-ba) and relaxing with presence (lhug-pa), come under the heading of stabilizing the practice, whereas the third essential instruction, progressing in the practice (bogs dbyung), is the third of the three topics we indicated above.

In terms of integration, the practice described here is integrating into the space of the sky (nam-mkhar ar-gtad). This is quite different from fixating on an object of meditation. That is working with the mind and contemplation lies beyond the mind. Here, after focusing our attention on a point in space, we relax and allow our awareness to integrate with the sky.

Second, there are some instructions for relaxing alertly with presence (lhug-pa) in general. The principle in Dzogchen is relaxation, but this relaxing is never dull or drowsy, as, for example, it is with a cow in the field chewing on its cud. That state of mind is called *lung ma bstan;* it is not *rig-pa.* Relaxing with presence means that when our senses have contact with some object, we do not enter into any conceptualizing about or judging of that object. We just let it be as it is. This is not a question of fixating attention acutely on some object of meditation or of trying to repress extraneous thoughts. In fact, we would soon discover that such a repression is virtually impossible. The more we try to repress thoughts, the more energy they absorb and they come back at us with a vengance. In terms of Dzogchen, it does not matter whether discursive thoughts (rnam-rtog) arise or not, so long as we are not distracted by them and do not follow after them. Our real problem is how to leave things well enough alone, and not try to modify and correct (ma bcos-pa) the thoughts which do arise.

However, when we continue to practice contemplation, certain problems may arise due to drowsiness or agitation. There are ways to handle these problems. Also, certain experiences may arise during practice, especially experiences of pleasurable sensation (bde-ba'i nyams), of clarity and luminosity (gsal-ba'i nyams), and of emptiness or nondiscursiveness (mi rtog-pa'i nyams). We should not confuse these experiences with contemplation or *rig-pa,* nor let them distract us. They are only experiences and nothing more. When we relax our body, speech, and mind, then our energies are released from the tight hold we usually maintain over them and so they begin to manifest freely and spontaneously. We may see beautiful visions, hear sounds, feel strange, and so on. But we should be aware that all of them are only manifestations of our energy and not be carried away by them. This is how to progress in the practice.

Then there is the practice of the night. Here there are two sections: the practice of the evening (srod kyi rnal-'byor) just before we fall asleep and the practice of the morning (tho-rangs rnal-'byor) as soon as we come awake. The practice of the evening is also known as the practice of the natural Clear Light ('od gsal).

The process of falling asleep is in many ways analogous to the process of dying. In the moment when we fall asleep, but before the onset of dreaming, we may have an experience of the Clear Light which is the clear luminosity of our primordial state. If we recognize this Clear Light, we can attain liberation at the end of this present life by integrating into it. The procedure spoken of here is a very effective method for remaining present while falling asleep. Its proximate effect is to produce lucid dreams, that is, we are aware that we are dreaming while we are in the dream state. Because we are aware of our dreams, we are then able to develop and transform them and use them as the basis of our practice. Although there are many complicated methods spoken of in the Tantras for the practice of dream yoga, this method of the natural Clear Light is quite simple and direct, and it achieves the same results.

The practice in the morning is a form of Guru Yoga. As we have said, in Dzogchen, every practice one does is linked with Guru Yoga. Through the method given here, we are able to awaken in the morning into a state of presence and awareness. We should understand that this very state of *rig-pa* into which we awaken is identical with the state of the Guru or master. In truth, it is none other than our own primordial state which is called Samantabhadra.

Finally, the author considers the benefits (phan-yon) of these practices and the qualities of a practitioner (rnal-'byor-pa'i yon-tan). Then there is the conclusion consisting of a dedication of merit (bsngo-ba) and a benediction (bkra-shis).

Although brief and concise, this upadeśa or secret essential instruction from a living master of Dzogchen to interested practitioners clearly indicates how to enter into the state of contemplation and how to progress in that state both during the day and during the night, so that the whole of our existence may become integrated into contemplation. It is the hope of the translator that this translation will prove of practical use to all who are interested.

SARVA MANGALAM

Notes to the Introduction

(1) *Upadeśa,* Tib. *man-ngag:* Fundamentally this term means "a secret oral instruction" communicated in private by a master to a disciple. Nowadays, the upadeśas of Tibetan masters are often preserved in written form. But it should not be forgotten that originally all of the Buddha's teachings were oral and written down some one hundred years after His passing into final Nirvāṇa.
(2) There are four principal schools of Tibetan Buddhism extant today: the Nyingmapa, the Sakyapa, the Kagyudpa, and the Gelugpa. Although they all hold the same fundamental doctrines of Mahāyaña Buddhism, there exist many differences with regard to lineage and emphasis on the practice of certain Tantras. Of these schools, the Nyingmapa is the oldest and preserves Buddhist traditions which come from the early period of translation, 7-9 cen. C.E. The other schools came into existence later with the renewal of translation activity in the 11 cen. C.E. Although nowadays a Tibetan Lama will usually be affiliated with one or the other of these four schools in terms of his ordinations and monastic lineage, in addition he will hold many lineages of initiation and teaching from masters who are not strictly members of his own school. We should not think of these schools and lineages of transmission as being mutually exclusive, like the Christian denominations and churches in the West.
(3) The Tibetan term Lama (bla-ma) translates the Sanskrit word Guru, or spiritual master and guide. Traditionally, there are said to be three kinds of Lamas: 1. the Gurus of the lineage (brgyud-pa'i bla-ma). That is, the various masters of all the teaching and initiation lineages of transmission (brgyud-pa) which one has received; 2. the Gurus who have given guidance ('dren-pa'i bla-ma), that is, all of the teachers one has had, at one time or another, in this

present life; and 3. one's Root Guru (rtsa-ba'i bla-ma) who is that master who has introduced one to the nature of his own mind, and who has given one the most important initiations and secret instructions for his spiritual development in this lifetime. This Root Guru has three aspects in terms of profundity: 1. the outer Guru (phyi'i bla-ma) is the actual master who initiates and instructs one, 2. the inner Guru (nang gi bla-ma) is one's own personal meditation deity (yi-dam) with whom one is especially linked throughout this present lifetime; and 3. the Secret Guru (gsang-ba'i bla-ma) is Samantabhadra, the primordial Buddha, who is none other than the nature of one's own mind.

(4) See below.

(5) *Bairo'i rgyud 'bum,* vol. V, 223-245; Leh, Ladakh, 1971.

(6) See below.

(7) The term Trikāya (Tib. sku gsum) in the Sūtra system refers only to the goal of the spiritual path, and not to the Base and the Path as well as it does in Dzogchen. As the goal, it means the manifestation of the full enlightenment of a Buddha in terms of his three Bodies (kāya) or dimensions of existence. The Dharmakāya (chos-sku) or "Reality Body" is beyond conception by the intellect and expression in words. It is the omnipresent all-pervading ultimate reality. The Sambhogakāya (longs-sku), "the body of enjoyment," manifests outside time and history in Akaniṣṭha, the highest plane of existence. Only the great Bodhisattvas whose faculties are entirely purified are able to perceive this glorious form. The Nirmāṇakāya (sprul-sku), "the emanation body," is the Buddha who appears in time and history as a teacher of the path. The historical Buddha Śākyamuni is just such a Nirmāṇakāya. Also, this term Nirmāṇakāya or Tulku is applied to the recognized reincarnations of great spiritual masters.

(8) On these preliminary practices, see note 3 in the Notes to the Text.

(9) The country of Uddiyāna (Tib. u-rgyan) was the principal place of origin of the Anuttara Tantras, as well as the Tantras of Dzogchen. It was the homeland of King Jah (dzah) to whom were first revealed the Mahāyoga Tantras, and also of Garab Dorje, the first human teacher of Dzogchen according to the Buddhist tradition (see below). Furthermore, Uddiyāna was the birth place of Padmasambhava, the master who established the Tantric form of Buddhism in Tibet. Some Western scholars, such as G. Tucci, would locate Uddiyāna in the Swat Valley of Pakistan. There exists some Tibetan evidence for this, particularly, the account of Urgyanpa. However, in ancient times, the geographical term Uddiyāna may have designated a rather wide area in northwest Pakistan and Afghanistan, and even in Western Tibet.

(10) These two systems are known as *mdo lugs,* "the Sūtra system," and *sngags lugs,* literally "the Mantra system," this being the usual designation of the system of the Tantras. In Sanskrit, this is *Mantrayāna,* not Tantrayāna, or something like that.

(11) *Śabda-mahāprasaṇga Tantra, Tib. sGra thal 'gyur gyi rgyud:* This is the chief among the seventeen Tantras of the Dzogchen Upadeśa series.
(12) *Kulayarāja Tantra, Tib. Kun-byed rgyal-po'i rgyud.* This is the chief among the Dzogchen semde Tantras.
(13) On the three types of transmission and on the various lineages of Dzogchen teaching, see *The Pure Melodious Voice of the Dragon* by Kunkhyen Longchenpa, translated with introduction and notes by Vajranātha (forthcoming).
(14) The term *Dhyāni Buddhas,* used to designate these five Tathāgatas or Buddhas who collectively embody the Sambhogakāya dimension of Buddhahood, is something of more recent Nepali Buddhist coinage. It is not found attested in either Sanskrit or Tibetan sources. It was introduced in the West by B. Hodgson in his writings about the Buddhism he observed being practiced in Kathmandu in the 1830's. Nonetheless, it is a convenient term to designate these five Buddhas. The word dhyāni would be derived from dhyāna, "meditation."
(15) The career of a Bodhisattva is marked by ten stages or *bhūmis* (sa bcu). Those who have attained the seventh through tenth stages are known as great Bodhisattvas. The attainment of the seventh stage represents irreversibility; one cannot fall back thereafter from the path to Buddhahood.
(16) The name Garab Dorje (dGa'-rab rdo-rje) is the Tibetan translation of an original which is nowhere attested in the extant literature, so far as we know. A number of Sanskrit reconstructions have been proposed, such as Praharshavajra, Pramadavajra, and so on. But since the form Prahevajra occurs in mantra invoking Garab Dorje in a Guru Yoga text by Dzogsar Khyentse Chokyi Lodro, we have elected to use this form as the most likely Sanskrit and Uddiyāna original. In any event, it could not be Ānandavajra, which in Tibetan is *dGe-ba'i rdo-rje.*
(17) According to the Phug-lugs system of Tibetan astrology and chronology, 2867 years have passed since the Mahāparinirvāna of the Buddha until the present year of 1986 C.E. This would place the passing of the Buddha in the year 881 B.C. Western scholars generally follow the Theravādin tradition of Śri Lanka (Ceylon) and accept the dates 566-486 B.C. for the Buddha. If Garab Dorje (Prahevajra) was born 166 years after the Mahāparinirvāṇa of the Buddha, as is asserted to be the case by Dudjom Rinpoche, then he was born in the year 715 C.E. However, according to the Kagyudpa historian Pawo Tsuk-lak (dPa'-bo gtsug-lag phreng-ba) in his *mKhas-pa'i dga'-ston,* Garab Dorje was born some 360 years after the passing of the Buddha. The version of the life of Garab Dorje presented here, principally follows the account given in the second chapter of Dudjom Rinpoche's *Bod snga rabs snying-ma'i chos-byung lha-dbang g-yul las rgyal-ba'i rnga-bo-che'i sgra dbyangs.* This version is also found

in *The Tantric Tradition of the Nyingmapa* by Tulku Thondup (Buddhayana, Marion, MA, 1984), pp. 46-52. See also *The Rise of Esoteric Buddhism in Tibet* by Eva Dargyay (Motilal Banarsidass, Delhi, 1977), pp. 16-26. There is a rather different version given in *Crystal Mirror V* by Tarthang Tulku (Dharma Press, Berkeley, 1977); but no Tibetan sources are cited here for this account. We have chosen to Sanskritize the proper names in the account here and use the name Prahevajra throughout, principally for reasons of euphony and consistency.

(18) The five syllables of this mantra refer to the five Dhyāni Buddhas (i.e., the Sambhogakāya). The glorious white male figure, no doubt He is Vajrasattva, consecrates the bhikshunī with the vase initiation (bum dbang) which purifies her body of all obscurations.

(19) A Dākinī, Tib. *mkha'-'gro-ma,* "she who goes in the sky," is the embodiment of wisdom in female form, the female aspect of the principle of enlightenment. There are wisdom or jñāna Dākinīs, who are fully enlightened beings, such as the great Bodhisattva Tārā; but also worldly or karma Dākinīs, which are female manifestations of energy in the world. Also, an accomplished female practitioner of the Dharma is known as a Dākinī. For certain esoteric yoga practices known as secret conduct (gsang spyod), the yogin must have as his partner in practice a Dākinī possessing all the requisite marks.

(20) This is the name of a famous Dzogchen Tantra. Prof. Norbu is preparing a wide-ranging study of this text.

(21) The term Tīrthika (mu-stegs-pa), "he who crosses (the stream) by a different ford," generally means a Hindu. A Brāhmana is a Brahmin priest of the Hindus and a Paṇḍuta is a Sanskrit scholar, whether Hindu or Buddhist.

(22) The Asuras are titanic beings who live in great caverns beneath the earth. They are in constant warfare with the Devas, or gods in heaven, over the great tree which possesses the fruits of eternal life.

(23) The Garuda, the highest flying among all birds, is a symbol for the non-gradual path of Dzogchen because it springs forth fully grown from the shell of its egg.

(24) Vajrāsana (Tib. rdo-rje gdan), "the diamond throne," refers to the site of the Buddha's enlightenment beneath the Bodhi tree. This site is now known as Bodh Gaya in the Indian state of Bihar. Some miles distant to the east is the cremation ground of Kolashri, which the Tibetans identify with the ancient site of Śītavana (bsil-ba'i tshal).

(25) The five traditional sciences are grammar, logic, art, medicine, and religious science.

(26) For a translation of this text, see *The Wise and Glorious King,* together with a commentary on the text by Patrul Rinpoche, translated with introduction and notes by Vajranātha (forthcoming).

(27) The precise location of this site is unknown, as is the proper Sanskrit form of the name.

(28) *'Ja'-lus* is the term for the "Rainbow Body" and one who has attained it is a *'ja'-lus-pa*. This is a method where, at the end of one's life, one can transform his physical body into pure radiant energy and vanish like a rainbow in the sky. This takes one beyond the cycle of transmigration, and one can choose to reappear in a body of light whenever one chooses in order to help and teach sentient beings. A number of Rainbow Bodies have been historically attested in Tibet in recent decades. Over the course of seven days the physical body of the adept actually shrinks away to nothing, leaving behind only nails and hair.

(29) Khri-srong lde'u btsan (b. 742 C.E.). Scholars disagree over the precise dates of these early kings of Tibet. For a generally reliable chronology, see D. Snellgrove and H. Richardson, *A Cultural History of Tibet*, (Boston: Shambhala, 1986), pp. 288-89.

(30) *Sad-mi mi bdun.*

(31) Prof. Norbu is preparing a definitive study of this text.

Garab Dorje

The Cycle of Day and Night

In the Tibetan language: *gDod-ma'i rnal-'byor gyi lam khyer nyin mtshan 'khor-lo-ma.*

In the English language: "The Cycle of Day and Night Where One Proceeds Along the Path of the Primordial Yoga"

Homage to the Master.

(1) I pay homage with great devotion of my three gates (of body, voice, and mind) to all the Masters of the Dzogchen Lineage, such as Changchub Dorje, who encompasses within himself all of the Buddha Families, as well as Urgyen Tenzin and Dorje Paldron. (2) The Primordial Buddha Samanătabhadra and the glorious Vajrasattva transmitted the method for proceeding along the path of the essence of Atiyoga to Garab Dorje, the supreme teacher. Desiring to explain a little of the nectar of this teaching, I entreat the Dākinīs to grant me their permission.

(3) We should always train our minds with the fourfold change of attitude and we should never separate ourselves from that yoga in which we are aware of our own innate presence as being our true Master. Continuing with this mindful awareness without distraction in the four moments (of eating, sitting, walking, and sleeping) is the root of the practice.

(4) Certainly, with respect to the day and the night, there does exist a principal daily practice which proceeds as a continuous cycle. The practice of the day which governs the activities of the three moments (of eating, sitting, and walking) is comprised of three topics: understanding, stabilizing, and progressing in the practice.

(5) (With respect to the first of these three topics): at the outset, we should understand what we have not yet understood. All phenomena which are either seen or heard, however many of them there may be, are like so many false images, even though they may appear to be very diverse. Thus we can conclusively determine that they are merely a magical display of the mind. (6) The nature of the mind is from the very beginning empty and without a self. Having nothing concrete about it, its aspect which is luminous clarity is unobstructed (and uninterrupted), like the moon reflected on the water. This is that ultimate primal awareness of pure presence within which there is no duality of emptiness and clarity. We should understand that this primal awareness is naturally and spontaneously self-perfected.

(7) Since we recognize that (external) appearances are merely ornaments (or embellishments) of the real condition of existence, appearances which arise to the alertly relaxed six sense aggregates are self-liberated into their own condition (whenever they arise). Since we recognize that pure presence is just primal awareness as such, manifestations of our passions and karmic traces are self-liberated into their own condition (whenever they

arise). (8) Since appearances and pure presence are recognized to be inseparable, thoughts which grasp at the duality of subject and object are self-liberated into their own condition (whenever they arise). Furthermore, the methods of self-liberation through bare attention, self-liberation upon the arising of thoughts, and self-liberation as such, are the means for progressing along the path of practice according to the intent of this yoga.

(9) The awareness arising at the first sudden instant (of sense contact) is indeed that pure presence which arises without correction (or modification) and which is uncreated (by causes). This very condition of existence which transcends the limitations of both subject and object is the authentic self-originated primal awareness of pure presence. (10) With respect to this pure presence, the three aspects of the state of Samantabhadra are truly complete: being devoid of any karmic traces, its Essence which is the Dharmakāya is emptiness; being devoid of thoughts and concepts, its Nature which is the Sambhogakāya is clarity; being devoid of any desires or attachments, (its Energy) which is the Nirmāṇakāya, is unobstructed (and uninterrupted).

(11) Such an awareness, in just its coming into being, is entirely devoid of dualistic thoughts which think in terms of subject and object, and so (external appearances) arise as manifestations of clarity without any grasping (at conceptions or judgments). Appearances present themselves in the state of the real condition of existence. (12) Because this unconditioned, natural, instantaneous awareness encounters the real condition of existence as its Mother, (we speak of it as) the Dharmakāya. Remaining in this condition of spontaneously self-perfected pure presence is the natural state of the Great Perfection.

(13) With respect to stabilizing (our practice, which is the second topic): we proceed along the path by way of the three

instructions for integrating, for relaxing with presence, and for progressing in the practice. As for the first method, that of integrating: while sitting comfortably and being completely relaxed, we integrate (our awareness) into the sky in front of ourselves. (14) When we settle thus into an alert, relaxed state without distraction and without constructed meditation, this initial awareness which is like (the clear empty) sky is also a condition devoid of any attachments or grasping (at conceptions and judgments). It is just luminous clarity or just pure presence, and it is similar to a moment of surprised astonishment. This pure presence arises in a bare and naked fashion without duality or distinction between the calm state and the movement of thoughts.

(15) While continuing in contemplation, without falling under the power of either drowsiness or agitation, we find ourselves in a state which is present in profound lucidity and vividness. With regard to continuing in a state of contemplation, even though we may engage in calling up thoughts, thrusting them aside, causing them to repeat, or expanding upon them, they remain in their own condition (whenever they arise) without our being distracted, and are self-liberated.

(16) After having attained this state, when we arise from the period of contemplation, the measure of our stability (in the practice) is our discerning whether or not we are subject to the power of conditioning thoughts. Experiences during meditation (arise spontaneously), like the rising of the light of the sun or of the moon. These experiences, such as visions, changes in breathing, and so on, as they arise are unconditioned by conceptions (or judgments). (17) As for experiences which appear after the period of contemplation: we may see all appearances as being illusions, or we may consider every appearance to be empty. (We may be capable of remaining) in a state of pure presence and it seems that no discursive thoughts arise, or we may think we can engage in activities without making any mistakes.

(18) As for our entire dimension: because of perceiving external objects and their analyses (on the one hand), and vivid and discursive thoughts (on the other hand), as empty, we attain the supreme Dharmakāya, which is the nature of mind. Since this (condition) is in no way contaminated by thoughts, characteristics, or cognitions, we come to attain a pure primal awareness unsullied by discursive thoughts. (19) Since our obscurations and karmic traces are now completely purified, our passions are no longer out of control. Because this is the case, even though we may be (ordinary individuals), we now find ourselves raised higher than all the realms of saṃsāra, and we are known to belong to the family of the Exalted Ones (Arhats).

(20) As to the instructions for relaxing with presence: whenever appearances arise, in whatever way they may arise, without any correction or modification, (we should look upon them) as mere ornaments or embellishments of the primordial state itself (which is the real condition of existence). In that state, our internal pure presence is uncorrected, clear, vivid, and naked. Thus, while relaxing alertly with presence, (when thoughts arise) we relax them into their own condition just as it is.

(21) With respect to the objects of the six sense faculties: when they simply arise as ornaments (of the state of presence) in a lucid fashion without any obstruction and without any intellectual analyses, then they are entirely perfect just as they are, as the potency of pure presence without any grasping (after conceptions or judgments). Continuing in this state without any duality is said to be relaxing with presence.

(22) While continuing in the period of contemplation, without engaging in any analyses of the objects of the five senses, (appearances are allowed) to arise clearly and luminously in an alertly relaxed fashion without any distraction or grasping (after conceptions and judgments). Then, after having concluded a period of contemplation, a primal awareness will present itself which is based on one or another of the objects of the six sense

aggregates; any such appearances (whether material or not) will seem to have no concrete reality. (23) Whenever discursive thoughts engendered by the five poisons arise, we alertly relax in the face of them without grasping (at conceptions or judgments). (On the other hand) we should not try to block them with some antidote or transform them by means of some method. (Since they are neither blocked nor transformed), the passions which arise on the path are self-liberated and a primal awareness is present.

(24) Experiences arising during meditation practice manifest as clarity and emptiness. They are found present in a state of vision and emptiness, or in a state of the continuing movement of thoughts and emptiness, or in a state of pleasurable sensation and emptiness, and so on. Thus, there may arise various conscious experiences of the presence of pleasurable sensation, of clarity, and of nondiscursiveness.

(25) As for our entire dimension: understanding all phenomena as the Dharmakāya, this uncorrected awareness of the state of existence as it is in itself is present like a perfect sphere which is uniform, whole, and without duality. Because of this, (it is said that) we have attained the dimension of primordial awareness, and a primal awareness of clarity is present.

(26) Since objects which we perceive are actually manifestations of the real condition of existence, our passions and obscurations become purified. Because this primal awareness of pure presence is present, we disentangle ourselves from engaging in any sort of negative behavior. And since we have become liberated from our passions, karmic traces, and obscurations, we are known to belong to the family of the noble Bodhisattvas.

(27) As for progressing in the practice (which is the third topic to be considered): in an uncorrected, spontaneously self-perfected state, this initial instantaneous awareness remains

present and unmodified. It is a nondiscursive pure presence which is lucid and vivid. Thus our continuity of awareness remains stable and undistracted. (28) While continuing in a period of contemplation, neither influenced by drowsiness nor by agitation, everything manifests itself as emptiness, which is the real condition of existence. Then, after having concluded a period of contemplation, without being conditioned by thoughts, we should continue in the state of the nature of mind, just as it is in itself.

(29) With respect to experiences during meditation, we find ourselves in a nondual state, whether we are meditating or *not meditating.* All appearances arise entirely as the manifestation of the energy of our contemplation. The real condition of the existence of all phenomena, just as they are, presents itself without moving from the naturally occurring primordial situation.

(30) As for our entire dimension: all phenomena, whether visible or invisible, are entirely purified of themselves in the state of the real condition of existence. Therefore, we attain the supreme dimension of nonduality, and a supreme primal awareness which is in no way clothed (in mental activities) is present. (31) Through completely purifying our obscurations to knowledge, we thus attain a knowledge of all phenomena just as they are in the real condition of their existence. Since we are entirely liberated from any duality in relation to the one who understands and that which is understood, we are known to belong to the family of the omniscient Tathāgatas.

(32) Now, with respect to proceeding along the path through the practice of the night, here we should train ourselves in two practices: one in the evening when we fall asleep and the other in the morning when we awaken again. In the evening (before falling asleep) we should allow our sense faculties to settle into a condition of continuous contemplation. Furthermore, we should integrate our practice of concentration with our sleep.

(33) At the moment of falling asleep, we should visualize a white letter A or a small sphere of five colored lights in the space between the eye brows. This is visualized clearly as being just about the size of a pea. First we fix our awareness on this; then we relax our awareness a bit and allow ourselves to fall asleep.

(34) When we fall asleep in a state in which the six sense aggregates are alertly relaxed into their own condition, our awareness does not become polluted by the grime of discursive thoughts and the natural clear light appears. We thus find ourselves in the presence of the real condition of existence without any discursive thoughts (distracting us).

(35) Or then again, when we observe this instantaneous awareness (at the moment it arises), we cannot see anything whatsoever in it that can be identified as calm or the movement of thought. Thus, finding ourselves in a state of alert, vibrant presence, we settle into a quiet awareness and fall asleep.

(36) The process of falling asleep is the cause of our entering into the clarity of the real condition of existence. (Our senses) are then absorbed completely into the Dharmadhātu in a state of pure presence. For as long as we are falling asleep, it is possible to continue finding ourselves being present in the state of just that real condition of existence. (37) Having become entirely disengaged from our karmic traces of a material body, our karmic traces of vision, and our karmic traces of mental activity, no further mental activity will arise (prior to the onset of dreaming.) We continue to find ourselves in the presence of the state of the real condition of existence. Thus, we will experience a certain degree of merging with the natural clear light.

(38) (At the moment when we actually) fall asleep, no discursive thoughts whatsoever will arise and our state of pure presence is absorbed into its Mother (the natural clear light) and we find ourselves present in the state of the real condition of existence. Subsequent to this period of contemplation (which is the natural clear light), we will come to recognize our dreams to be merely dreams when we enter into the dream state. Finding

ourselves freed of all illusions, (dreams) manifest in a helpful friendly fashion as our dimension and our primordial awareness.

(39) In the early morning, (immediately upon awakening), a primal awareness arises which is uncorrected and present in its own condition. If we remain in this natural state without distraction and without meditating on anything, then we will find ourselves quietly present, undisturbed by any discursive thoughts. This is known as the state of the Guru Samantabhadra.

(40) Looking directly into the face of that state (of pure presence), we observe with bare attention who it is that is meditating. Not finding anything recognizable (or confirmable) there, a lucid and naked self-originated primal awareness self-liberates as it arises. Then a nondual primal awareness becomes present. (41) At that moment, finding ourselves beyond all objective vision, and transcending all discursive thoughts which grasp at duality, a primal awareness of nondiscursiveness becomes clearly manifest. Since we are aware, a primal awareness of clarity, unsullied (by the taint of discursive thoughts), becomes clearly manifest. Since there is no duality (of subject and object present), a primal awareness of pleasurable sensation becomes clearly manifest. (42) Since we have come to understand that all phenomena are in themselves actually the real condition of existence, a primal awareness which is in no way mistaken becomes supremely manifest. And since a primal awareness of quantity (which knows each thing in its individuality) becomes clearly manifest in its entirety, the inherent nature of the three dimensions of our existence becomes supremely manifest.

(43) When one practices the essence of this yoga both day and night, the whole of our dimension of life enters into contemplation. Becoming familiar with the practice, our passions will arise on the path (as something useful to us). Certainly we will attain the full measure of accomplishing the benefit of beings, whose numbers are equal to the vastness of the sky, because of

realizing the three dimensions of our existence. (44) The measure of our familiarity (with this practice is the degree to which we are able to) recognize our dreams to be dreams while we are still asleep. Since attachments to sensations of pleasure and pain (will be overcome day by day), we find ourselves in a state of integration, in no way clothed (in concepts or judgments). Because primal awareness is present, all appearances arise as friends (who can help us on the path). The continuity of illusion is thus interrupted and we find ourselves in the presence of the state of the real condition of existence. (45) Since the practitioner of Atiyoga, throughout both the day and the night, remains without moving from this state of the real condition of existence, it is said that he or she may realize Buddhahood even in the instant between two breaths. So it was said by that great being Garab Dorje.

(46) With regard to the passions arising on the path (as something useful in our practice), without categorizing phenomena (as either good or bad), we find them present in the state of the real condition of existence. Because all of them are present in total awareness, without there being any conceptualizing with regard to them, we recognize delusion (itself as being nothing other than) nondiscursiveness. Phenomena manifest (nondiscursively) as the real condition of existence just as it is in itself. (47) All phenomena which appear as objects of the six sense aggregates are present in luminous clarity and lacking in any inherent nature. Because of that, we recognize anger to have the character of clarity and it manifests now as the primal awareness of clarity. (48) Everything which manifests externally is the real condition of existence, while internally, pure presence is primal awareness. Because the sensation of great bliss, which is without any dualistic distinctions, has the nature of Energy, we recognize desires to represent in actuality the potency of great bliss. There thus manifests a primal awareness of the sensation of great bliss which is spontaneously self-perfected without any limitations.

(49) Moreover, other beings are benefitted by way of the three dimensions of our existence. Furthermore, the three poisonous passions manifest themselves entirely as the dimension of our existence and its inherent primordial awareness. And because of that, everything which arises from them is present also as our dimension of existence and its inherent primordial awareness. (50) Because what we call 'passions' no longer exist, no further causes for transmigrating in saṃsāra exist. With respect to that, even though we may think to call this condition "nirvāṇa," in reality it is simply the multitude of virtuous qualities (of our primordial state of Buddhahood) spontaneously manifesting themselves in self-perfection, without any corrections or modifications being made to them. Like the sun rising in the sky, we may say that this is just clarity as such.

(51) With respect to this method: the sphere of activity of students should embrace the five capacities of willingness to participate, diligence, mindful presence, concentration, and intelligence. In accordance with whatever instructions we have received from the supreme vehicle (of Atiyoga), we should know how to realize for ourselves the harmonious conditions for completing and perfecting (these five capacities).

(52) Having stated all this, by virtue of these few succinct words which give a little of the nectar of the state of the Master Kunzang Garab Dorje, may I and all other beings, equal in numbers to the vastness of the sky, who are linked with me (karmically and spiritually), come quickly to attain the very status of the victorious Jina Samantabhadra!

This text, which is intended for those who desire to participate in the supreme vehicle of Dzogchen, was set down in memory of Mr. Paul Anderson, who has passed away peacefully. Because we are beginning a retreat at the Dzogchen Community of Conway in the eastern part of America, this text was written by the Dzogchen practitioner Namkhai Norbu in the year of the Water-Pig in the ninth month on the third day, which is surely a day of good fortune!

Conway, Massachusetts
October 9, 1983

At the request of Namkhai Norbu Rinpoche and in collaboration with the members of the Dzogchen Community of Conway, this text on the continuous practice of Dzogchen contemplation was translated into the English language by Vajranatha, John Myrdhin Reynolds.

SARVA MANGALAM

Chang Chub Dorje

Topical Outline of the Text

Notes to the Text Based on the Oral Commentary of Namkhai Norbu

Title: The title of this text in Tibetan is *gDod-ma'i rnal-'byor gyi lam khyer nyin mtshan 'khor-lo-ma.* "Primordial Yoga" (gdod-ma'i rnal-'byor) refers to the knowledge of the primordial state of the individual which is called in Tibetan *rig-pa* "pure presence, intrinsic awareness." Primordial Yoga is a synonym for Atiyoga and for Dzogchen. The latter term is usually translated as "the Great Perfection" (rdzogs-pa chen-po). Here this teaching is put into practice (lam khyer, "proceeding along the path"). Since this is not just a retreat practice, but one which is practiced in a continuous fashion both day and night (nyin mtshan), it is said to be like a wheel ('khor-lo).

I. The Salutation

(1) The title is followed by the salutation to the Masters and by two verses of invocation (mchod brjod). Here the author invokes his own Root Master, Changchub Dorje of Nyala Gar in Derge,

East Tibet. It was this Master who revealed to the author the essential meaning of Dzogchen in terms of immediate experience as opposed to mere intellectual comprehension. He then invokes the name of his uncle Urgyan Tenzin, who was his first Master, and the name of Dorje Paldron (Ayu Khandro) who conferred upon him the Dzogchen Yangti precepts and other teachings.

(2) All teachings are linked to their transmission (brgyud-pa). In the case of Dzogchen, these teachings originate with the Primordial Buddha Samantabhadra (Kun-tu bzang-po) who is the Dharmakāya aspect of Enlightenment. He transmitted them in a direct fashion mind-to-mind (dgongs brgyud) to Vajrasattva (rDo-rje sems-dpa') who is the Sambhogakāya aspect of Enlightenment. He in turn transmitted them in a symbolic fashion (brda brgyud) to the first human teacher of Dzogchen, Prahevajra or Garab Dorje (dGa'-rab rdo-rje), who is the Nirmanakāya aspect. Garab Dorje transmitted the teachings orally (snyan brgyud) to Manjuśrīmitra and to the Dākinīs (mkha'-'gro-ma), who are the custodians of these teachings, so that he may explain a little of the meaning of the Dzogchen precepts. These enlightened female beings were responsible for compiling the Dzogchen precepts received from Garab Dorje into esoteric texts called Tantras. These Tantras are arranged in three series of texts: *Semde* (sems-sde) "the Mind Series," *Longde* (klong-sde) "the Space Series," and *Upadeśa* or *Mangagide* (man-ngag gi sde) "the Secret Instruction Series."

II. The Preliminary Practice

(3) In the beginning, we practitioners of Dzogchen should purify our mental continua or streams of consciousness (rgyud sbyang) by training our minds with the four meditations which bring about a change in our attitude toward life (blo ldog rnam bzhi). These four are: 1. the difficulty of obtaining a human rebirth, 2. the impermanence of life, 3. the universality of suffering in Saṃsāra, and 4. the causes and consequences of karma.

In practical terms, this means that no matter what practice we are doing, we have to be aware. For example, if we know how to perform some practice, such as prostrations, but because we are distracted or lazy, we avoid doing it, we must ask ourselves why does this happen? It happens because we are not aware, and to be aware means that we do not waste our time. Moreover, to be aware means that we ought to know the preciousness of the teaching and the unique opportunity we now have in this human existence of practicing the teaching. From this awareness arises the knowledge of the consequences of losing this unique opportunity (dal 'byor) afforded by this precious human existence (mi lus rin-po-che). All of this is involved in what we mean by being aware.

Usually, when we speak of these four meditations, we speak first of the importance of possessing a human rebirth. When we study the preliminary teachings or Ngondro (sngon 'gro), we learn the explanations of the eighteen characteristics (dal 'byor bco-brgyad) of a precious human existence one by one in detail. But equally, we should be aware that, even though we now find ourselves reborn on this planet earth as human beings, this situation is not something which is permanent and everlasting. In the Sūtras, the example is given of a merchant who, due to fortuitous circumstances, found himself on an island of jewels in the midst of the great ocean, but who returned home empty-handed because of his lack of awareness. When we eventually die and find ourselves in the Bardo, the state between death and rebirth, if we have gone through our entire life without awareness, being unaware of the preciousness of human existence and the impermanence of life, then our condition will be no better than that of a dog. Usually, in Buddhist texts there is found an elaborate analysis of the impermanence of the world and of the individual. However, the important point here is not memorizing a lot of analyses, but simply to have the presence of this awareness of impermanence with us at all times.

Nonetheless, even if we are aware of the impermanence of life, if we do not take any positive action with respect to this fact of existence, we will not accumulate any causes for a fortunate rebirth. We have ignored the exceedingly important fact of karma. If we simply continue to accumulate negative causes, then we are certain to experience negative consequences in the future. The end result of this will be transmigration and suffering in the different destinies of rebirth. When we become aware of the causes and consequences of our actions, and of the universality of suffering in Saṃsāra, then we will surely become motivated to practice the teachings of the Dharma, which is the sure and certain path to liberation and enlightenment.

Above all, to train ourselves in these four meditations means that we try to be present and aware at any given moment in any circumstance. This does not mean that we simply study Buddhist books or indulge ourselves in elaborate intellectual analyses. For example, there are some people who learn a Ngondro text in Tibetan and then practice the Ngondro for a long period of time. There is nothing wrong with this; the Ngondro is an exceedingly important practice. When they study these four meditations, they first learn how to analyze what are the requisite conditions of a precious human existence—this is a human existence where all the conditions for the practice of the Dharma are present.

What are these conditions? Firstly, one is free of eight conditions where one finds no opportunity or leisure to practice the Dharma. These are rebirth among the denizens of hell, rebirth among the Pretas or hungry ghosts, rebirth among the animals, rebirth among barbarians who have no knowledge of the Dharma, rebirth among the long-lived gods, rebirth among people who harbor wrong views, rebirth in an age in which no Buddha has appeared in the world, and rebirth in a human body which has its faculties impaired. These conditions are known as the eight states of unease (mi khom-pa brgyad) and their opposites are the eight opportunities (dal-ba brgyad). Secondly, there are ten favorable conditions ('byor-pa bcu) which are necessary, five due to another and five due to oneself. Among these, the five external conditions refer to the appearance of a

Buddha in the world: a Buddha has appeared in the world, He has taught the Dharma, His teaching is established and persists, one enters into the practice of the Dharma, and there exist other living beings in the world who may serve as the objects of one's compassionate actions. The five internal conditions are due to one's own situation: one is born as a human being, one is born in a country where one has access to the teachings, one is born with his faculties complete, one does not resort to wrong deeds or wrong livelihood, and one has faith in the master and his teaching. None of these conditions should be lacking.

Finally, when these individuals begin to practice in a retreat, *they are instructed by their master* to meditate on these analyses and arguments, one by one, for some eighteen days. Many practitioners have done this, and this is how it was intended to be done, that is, they meditated on each argument in turn concerning these eighteen requisite conditions for a precious human existence and trained themselves in this.

But in the Dzogchen teaching, awareness does not function in this way. We do not have to establish some argument and then confirm it. These arguments and schemes of analysis were created by later teachers. When the Buddha Śākyamuni spoke about the preciousness of a human existence and of its impermanence, He gave such examples as a cloud in the autumn sky, a mountain stream, a theatre production, a flickering flame of a butter lamp, and so on. Extracting these examples from the Sūtras or the discourses of the Buddha, scholars enumerated and analyzed them, and in this way, created a procedure for reasoning about the fact of impermanence. But the Buddha Himself did not go about constructing arguments based on His examples. What He was attempting to do was to bring different people to an understanding of the conditions of human existence by way of using various different methods. So the principle here is not meditating on these various arguments which seek to establish the impermanence of everything, including our own life, but to have with us at all times a presence of the awareness of the impermanence of all things. It is not important how our present human existence fulfills these eighteen requisite conditions—that is not the principle. Rather, we should simply be aware at all times of the unique opportunity afforded by a human rebirth, so that we do not waste that opportunity. Our human existence is better than that of a cat or a dog, for a human being knows how to think and how to use and understand language. A human being also has a far greater capacity for doing evil in this world than do cats and dogs, as for example, the creating of nuclear weapons. But human beings also have the capacity to realize enlightenment in this life, and thus their capacity is far superior to those of animals. This is the true significance of a human existence—our potential. Being aware of our real condition, both our limitations and our capacities, is what we mean by mindfulness and awareness (dran rig).

If we must study in detail in the texts all of these analyses, then the matter becomes very complicated, not only for Tibetans, but even more so for Westerners. In this way the real meaning often becomes lost. This must be avoided, and so it is necessary to simplify things in order to get at the actual principle involved. Awareness does not mean just these four meditations spoken of here; in principle it means not to be distracted, and to try to do one's best in any circumstance. This is the way to train ourselves in being aware and present. This is what is meant by "training the mind" (blo sbyong); and the above, these four meditations which bring about a change in our attitude, constitute the ordinary preliminary practice.

Then there are the extraordinary preliminary practices. The purpose of these practices is to accumulate meritorious karma (dge bsags) and to purify our obscurations (sgrib sbyong). These practices include going to refuge in the Three Jewels, generating the Bodhicitta or thought of enlightenment, the meditation and mantra recitation for Vajrasattva, the offering of the mandala, and the Guru Yoga or unification with all of the masters. The most important of these is the Guru Yoga.

Teachings such as Tantra and Dzogchen are linked to transmission. Transmission is a means to make the primordial state of the individual understood at the level of immediate experience, whether through words or symbols or directly mind to mind. The function of the Master (bla-ma) is to bring the practitioner to the realization that the nature of his mind (Sems-nyid) is like a mirror and the thoughts which arise in it are like the reflections which appear in this mirror. Our pure presence or intrinsic awareness (rig-pa) is like the capacity of that mirror to reflect everything which comes before it, whether beautiful or ugly. These reflections arise as characteristics or qualities of the mirror itself. But because the nature or capacity of this mirror is not seen, we mistake the reflections for something solid and externally real. Thus we become conditioned by these reflections, and acting on the basis of this false assumption, we fall again into transmigration. It is the Master who introduces (ngo-sprod) the practitioner to this distinction between mind or thoughts (sems) on the one hand and the Nature of the Mind (sems-nyid) on the other. When we begin to understand this, we can truly speak of a transmission of knowledge, knowledge not just in terms of intellectual comprehension, but of actual experience.

In the context of Dzogchen, the term yoga (rnal-'byor) does not simply mean "union" as it does ordinarily, but rather it refers to one who possesses ('byor-pa) a knowledge of his natural state (rnal-ma), that is to say, he finds himself in the presence of this knowledge of his primordial condition which is called *Rig-pa* or pure presence. This being aware (shes-pa) of one's own innate pure presence or intrinsic awareness (rig-pa) is our True Guru (bla-ma). The opposite of this condition is ignorance (ma rig-pa). We should not let ourselves be separated from this awareness at any time. The four moments or occasions (dus bzhi) referred to in the text are eating, walking, sitting, and sleeping. As we have said, in Dzogchen, the principal point is not to be distracted (ma yengs) and to continue in the presence of this mindful awareness (dran-shes). This is the root of the practice (rnal-'byor rtsa yin).

III. The Practice of the Day

(4) Generally, in our ordinary experience, what revolves continuously is the cycle (rgyun gyi 'khor-lor) of day and night. Therefore, there is a practice of the day (nyin-mo'i rnal-'byor) and a practice of the night (mtshan-mo'i rnal-'byor). With respect to the practice of the day, there are three principal topics to be considered: understanding the practice (rtogs-pa), stabilizing the practice (brtan-pa), and progressing in the practice (bogs dbyung).

A. Understanding the Practice

(5) The first of the three topics is understanding the practice. "Understanding" (rtogs-pa) is not just reasoning (brtag-pa) and analyzing (dpyad-pa), but it relies upon transmission. Our view (lta-ba) is a way of seeing or looking at things and it may include analysis and explanation. But "understanding" is fundamentally an entering into a knowlege of that view experientially. When we have no concrete knowledge of this sort, we are dependent upon the descriptions and interpretations of others, and these may change from day to day. Without real knowledge, all phenomena (chos kun) are merely false images (bden-med gzugs-brnyan); they do not exist in a real sense, but are like so many reflections in a mirror. A kitten, not knowing the image in the mirror is his own reflection, pursues it as if it were a real playmate. In Dzogchen, all appearances (snang-ba) are understood to be the potency (rtsal) of the energy of the Bodhicitta or the primordial state. These appearances are the qualifications or ornaments of that state. When we enter into knowledge we have no doubt of this. Thus we may conclusively determine (kho-thag-chod) that appearances are a magical display of the mind (sems kyi cho-'phrul).

(6) The Nature of the Mind (sems-nyid) is from the very beginning void or empty (stong-pa) and without any self or concrete substance (bdag-med). But we should not think of mind as being a mere nothing (med-pa) because it has the clarity and

limpidity of the mirror. This clarity (gsal-cha) exists unobstructedly and without interruption ('gags-med), just as the moon is reflected in the water in various ways. Thoughts arising in mind are the way in which the Nature of Mind manifests itself. But just as we must understand the reflections in order to understand the nature of the mirror, so we must examine thoughts to see where they arise, where they abide, and where they go. However, when we look into this matter, we discover that there is no place where thoughts arise or abide or go. Nothing can be affirmed and what we find is void or emptiness (stong-pa nyid). This is the real character of the mind. Now, even *though this may be the case, thoughts (rnam-rtog) continue to* arise without interruption ('gags-med). Therefore, what we find is a primal awareness of pure presence (rig-pa'i ye-shes) where there is no duality of emptiness (stong-pa nyid) on the one hand and clarity (gsal-ba) on the other. This primal awareness is natural and spontaneously self-perfected (rang-bzhin lhun-grub). At the level of mind (sems) we do not find this nonduality because mind operates in time, while the state of pure presence (rig-pa) lies beyond the limits of mind.

(7) When we recognize that appearances are merely ornaments of the real condition of existence (chos nyid rgyan), these appearances which arise to our alertly relaxed (lhug-pa) six senses are self-liberated into their own condition (rang sar grol) whenever they arise. The six sense aggregates (tshogs drug) are the five senses plus the mind (yid). The presence of appearances prior to forming any conception or judgment is called "clarity." Appearances (snang-ba) refer to the external world, whereas the passions or afflictions (nyon-mongs) and the karmic traces (bag-chags) refer to the world of inner experience. The manifestation of the internal state of pure presence is primal awareness (ye-shes). The arising of pure presence (rig-pa) never lacks its spontaneous self-perfection (lhun-grub), that is to say, its essential qualities, just as the rising sun does not lack its rays. Our passions only grow powerful because we are ignorant of the state of pure presence, and so consequently we follow after our

passions. But when we find ourselves in the state of the pure presence of the passions, they do not dominate us nor do we have to suppress them because they are like the ornaments of our primordial state. Thus our passions are self-liberated into their own condition (rang sar grol) whenever they arise.

(8) Appearances and pure presence are inseparable (snang rig dbyer-med). When we recognize (ngos zin) this and find ourselves in this state, then the discursive thoughts arising which grasp at the duality (gnyis su 'dzin-pa'i rnam-rtog) of subject and object, are liberated into their own condition (rang sar grol). We do not try to block or reject them in any way, but we simply remain aware in the presence of their arising. There are three procedures for self-liberation in this case, depending upon the capacity of the practitioner: 1. self-liberation through bare attention (gcer grol), 2. self-liberation upon the arising of a thought (shar grol), and 3. self-liberation as such (rang grol). The term *gcer* means "bare or naked attention." But this is not yet real self-liberation because, in observing ourselves, we are still applying some degree of effort. For example, when a thought arises, we look it straight in the face and it liberates into its own condition. The term *shar* means "to arise." At the moment the thought arises, it is self-liberated. For example, when we notice a thought arise, we do not have to make the effort to look it straight in the face, but just as it arises, we find ourselves in the state of presence which is Rig-pa and it self-liberates. True self-liberation (rang-grol) occurs when this capacity is fully developed. At this level, we have arrived at the continuity of the state of Rig-pa.

(9) This verse gives the essence of the matter. The awareness (shes-pa) arising at the first sudden instant (thol-'byung skad-cig dang-po) of sense contact is that pure presence (rig-pa) which is manifested without modification or correction (ma bcos) by the mind and which is not created or produced (skye-med) by any causes. What is this state of presence? It is a condition of existence (de-bzhin-nyid) transcending the limitations of both subject and object (gzung 'dzin mtha' las 'das-pa); it is a natural or authentic

(gnyug-ma) self-originated primordial awareness of pure presence (rang-byung rig-pa'i ye-shes). The term *de-bzhin-nyid* indicates the state characterized by both primordial purity (ka-dag) and spontaneous self-perfection (lhun-grub).

(10) Within this state of pure presence (rig-pa), the three Aspects (chos gsum) of the State of Samantabhadra (kun-bzang dgongs-pa) are wholly present. These three are termed the Essence, the Nature, and the Energy. With respect to the state of pure presence, its Essence (ngo-bo) which is the Dharmakāya (chos-sku) is emptiness (stong-pa-myid). This Essence is one, the essential Ground in which all phenomena are identical. *Dharma* (chos) means the whole of existence and *kāya* (sku) means the dimension of that. Since there do not exist any karmic traces or residues (bag-chags) in this state, we speak of its Essence as being emptiness. Karma is always something which belongs to the level of mind (sems), while pure presence or Rig-pa lies beyond the limited functioning of the mind. Thus we speak here not of mind (sems), but of primordial awareness or gnosis (ye-shes). Its Nature (rang-bzhin) which is the Sambhogakāya (longs-sku) is luminous clarity (gsal-ba). *Sambhoga* (longs-spyod rdzogs-pa) means possessing richness, enjoying all the qualities of Enlightenment in their perfection. *Kāya* (sku) means the dimension of that. Luminous clarity (gsal-ba) indicates that there is a manifestation as energy from the Primordial Ground which is emptiness; this manifestation is not yet material but it is differentiated and finds expression as the five primordial lights or awarenesses (ye-shes lnga). This dimension is beyond all conceptual constructions created by the finite intellect. Its Energy (thugs-rje) which is the Nirmāṇakāya (sprul-sku) is unobstructed and uninterrupted ('gags-med). *Nirmāṇa* (sprul-pa) means manifestation or emanation and *Kāya* (sku) means the dimension of that. Here "manifestation" means something at the relative level, that is to say, in contact with sentient beings in the material dimension. The Buddha Śākyamuni, who manifested in time and history, was just such a Nirmāṇakāya. However, the Nirmāṇakāya

is not conditioned by Karma (las) or by the passions (nyon-mongs). Thus the Trikāya (sku gsum), as Essence, Nature, and Energy, is wholly present from the very beginning in the self-perfected state of Rig-pa.

(11) This awareness (shes-pa) or pure presence (rig-pa) of which we speak here arises at the very first fresh instant before the mind has had a chance to come into operation, functioning dualistically in terms of subject and object. In this case, external appearances (snang-ba) arise merely as a manifestation of luminous clarity (gsal 'char). Everything that we are aware of arises through our senses: the six sense aggregates (tshogs drug)—the five physical senses plus mind (yid). When sense contact occurs, the presence of sensation is communicated to the mind (yid) and then a mental process ensues which engenders various conceptions and judgments. But when the mind has not yet entered into judgment or conceptualization, this is called *'dzin-med*, or being without grasping at anything. Without entering into any judgments, we remain present in awareness. Thus we say that appearances (snang-ba) are present or abide (gnas-pa) in the real condition of existence itself, the Dharmatā (chos-nyid). *Dharma* (chos) means "whatever exists" and *-ta* (nyid) means "in its own condition." All things which arise have their own inherent condition or nature (rang-bzhin). Different things may arise, yet their inherent condition is the same. For example, wood and water appear to be different and their functions present themselves differently, but their true inherent nature (rang-bzhin) is the same, namely, emptiness. This level of manifestation of the energy of all phenomena is called the Dharmatā. When we speak of the energy of the individual, we use the term *rtsal* to denote this energy of the condition of existence as it is. So we must understand what is meant by Dharmatā; otherwise we cannot integrate our own energy with it.

In conclusion, what is meant here is that when a thought arises in our minds, we do not enter into a judgment of it. However, this does not mean that we are drowsy or inattentive at that moment. Rather, we are absolutely present at that moment, totally aware and alert. And if we find ourselves present in that state of alertness, we will be beyond all dualistic concepts, and yet we will be there with the full presence of our senses. If we remain in this state of presence, even though someone is doing something near us, we need only make a mental note of it without following after that thought. The functioning of our senses is in no way blocked or impeded, but we do not let the mind enter into judgments about what is happening. Being in such a state of presence, we find ourselves in what is called the Dharmatā, the real condition of existence.

(12) Since this natural state of initial instantaneous awareness (skad-cig-ma yi shes-pa rnal-ma) *encounters as its own Mother* the real condition of existence (chos-nyid ma dang 'phrad-pas), we can say that, in truth, it is the Dharmakāya. What does this meeting with its own Mother mean? The Mother Dharmatā (chos-nyid ma) means the real condition of existence as it is, and from this all phenomena (chos) arise, just as children are born from their mother. In Tantra, we speak of everything arising out of Śūnyatā or emptiness, as for example, the wind element or vāyumandala arises, followed by the other elements in succession. Thus Śūnyatā or emptiness is the condition of things as such and we speak of this as *ka-dag*, "pure from the very beginning." Since everything arises from this Dharmatā, it is called "the Mother." In general, the individual is conditioned by his conceptions and by his dualistic view of the world. Moreover, he has no real understanding of what is meant by Śūnyatā without entering into reasoning and dualistic judgments. But here there is a meeting face to face with the Mother Wisdom of the Dharmatā and this does not involve any functioning of the mind, no reasoning or discursive thinking. We experience just this dimension of existence in itself which is the Dharmakāya. Dharmakāya does not mean an image of the Buddha, meditating with folded hands and crossed legs; the image of the Primordial Buddha Samantabhadra exists only to give the finite limited human intellect some idea of the meaning of the Dharmakāya. This image is a symbol, but the Dharmakāya in itself is actually beyond conception and

expression in terms of form, color, etc. It is the all-pervasive dimension of existence itself.

What is meant by mind (sems)? It must be distinguished from what is called the Nature of Mind (sems-nyid). To clarify matters, there is the example of the reflections in a mirror. The thoughts which arise in the mind are like the reflections, while the mirror itself, which has the capacity to reflect, is like the Nature of Mind. When thoughts arise, we do not follow after them and enter into judgments and conceptions (dmigs-pa), but we simply remain present and this quality of the Nature of Mind is called Rigpa. Rigpa means this state of presence. This Rigpa is also *lhun-grub,* that is to say, spontaneously self-perfected in all its qualities right from the very beginning. It is not a question of acquiring something we do not now possess. Rather, when we find ourselves in a state of presence, this state manifests all its inherent qualities spontaneously and this is what is meant by *lhun-grub.* This is the original natural authentic state of spontaneously self-perfected pure presence (rig-pa lhun-grub) which is the natural State of the Great Perfection (rdzogs-pa chen-po'i dgongs-pa rnal-ma). What does Dzogchen, "the Great Perfection," mean? It is not some text or tradition or sect or philosophical system. Rather, it is the primordial state of the individual, pure from the very beginning and spontaneously self-perfected. Finding ourselves in this state is called Dzogchen, the Great Perfection. When we are aware of this state, this is knowledge (rig-pa) and when we are not aware of it, this is ignorance (ma rig-pa).

B. *Stabilizing the Practice*

(13) The second topic here is "stabilizing our practice (brtan-pa)." We have now come to some understanding of the state of Rigpa which was what we had not understood previously. Next, we must train ourselves in finding ourselves in this state of presence. Being in the state of presence is called *samādhi* or contemplation (ting-nge-'dzin). In the Sūtras and the Tantras,

there are many methods given for this, but here there are three essential instructions (man-ngag gsum) to be considered: 1. integrating (bsre-ba), 2. relaxing with presence (lhug-pa), and 3. progressing in the practice (bogs dbyungs). These three are concerned with bringing presence into daily life. The first two of these instructions, integrating and relaxing with presence, come under the heading of stabilizing the practice, while the third instruction is the third topic among the three we are considering, namely, understanding, stabilizing, and progressing in the practice.

1. *Integrating*

First, we must consider the method for integrating (bsre-ba) or remaining in presence. Taking up a comfortable position and letting ourselves become relaxed (khong lhod) both externally and internally, without being charged up in any way, we integrate our awareness into the clear open space of the sky in front of us (mdun gyi mkha' ru ar la gtad). This practice is called *nam-khar ar-gtad.* Now, if we gaze at a fixed point, this is called "fixation," but that is not *ar-gtad* or integrating. Here there is no actual point in space upon which we fixate. Rather, when we gaze into the sky, in our way of looking it seems as if the sensation of our eyes vanishes into the openness of the sky. The openness of space is integrated with our state and we continue in that way. If we are just looking into the sky, this is called "looking into the sky;" but the term *ar-gtad* indicates that a process of re-integration of our energies is occurring, and that even though there is nothing to be done with the mind, still the mind is present there with a bare attention in the moment of our gazing into the sky.

(14) When we settle in this way into an alert relaxed state (lhug-par bzhag-pa) without distraction (yengs-med) and without constructed meditation (sgom-med), this initial awareness which is like the sky (shes-pa nam-mkha' ltar) is also a condition where we are without any attachments or grasping at conceptions and judgments ('dzin chags bral-ba'i ngang). Meditation involves

the functioning of the mind, and so it is not contemplation, which is beyond the mind. With respect to integrating into space (nam-mkhar ar-gtad), there is nothing to be done with the mind, nothing to be visualized or recited. We are not thinking about anything; what is present is simply a bare attention. This awareness (shes-pa) which is present there is like the sky and has nothing in it relating to mental creation or attachment. It is just a simple presence of clarity, and we continue in that.

It is similar to a moment of surprised astonishment (had-de-ba); as for example, when we hear a loud sharp sound nearby, all thought processes cease for a moment. Thereupon there arises a naked bare awareness (rig-pa rjen gcer shar) where there exists no duality or distinction between the calm state (gnas-pa) where no thoughts arise and the movement ('gyu-ba) of thoughts. Zhine (zhi-gnas) or Skt. *śamatha* is a calm state where discursive thoughts (rnam-rtog) are not present; however this condition is not what is meant by contemplation itself. Zhine is only an experience of calmness. When thoughts arise, this is the experience of the movement of thoughts. The state of Rigpa or pure presence is neither this calm nor this movement, but it is the presence which is found in both of these states.

(15) While continuing in the period of contemplation (mnyam-bzhag), without falling under the power of either drowsiness (bying-ba) or agitation (rgod-pa), we find ourselves in a state which is present in profound lucidity and vividness (sal-le hrig-ge ting-nger gnas-pa'i ngang). There exist many types of Śamatha or Zhine practice and also defects in this practice, such as drowsiness and agitation. In the Sūtra system, antidotes are given for these defects, but here it is explained that being in the state of Rigpa is beyond any such defects. In the state of Rigpa, right from the very beginning, there have never been any faults or defects. Thus, the principle here is that we find ourselves perfectly in that state. When this state is present, there is no drowsiness nor agitation; so it is not a question of applying antidotes to the defects. This is an important principle taught in the Dzogchen Upadeśa. When we continue in this state of presence, even

though we deliberately call up thoughts or repress them or cause them to repeat or expand upon them, they will remain in their own condition (rang sar gnas). Whenever they arise, without being distracted or moved from a state of presence, they will be self-liberated (rang grol). Even though all these thoughts may occur, this will in no way change or modify our state of presence.

(16) The period during which we continue in a state of contemplation is called *mnyam-bzhag,* while the time subsequent to attaining that state is called *rjes-thob.* When coming out of a period of contemplation, the measure of our stability in the practice (brtan-pa'i tshad) is the discovering whether or not we are subject to the power of conditioning thoughts (rkyen dbang). Until we come to remain all of the time in the state of the Great Contemplation, a period of contemplation will always be followed by a period of non-contemplation. However, even when we come out of contemplation, our pure presence or intrinsic awareness (rig-pa) will not be conditioned by discursive thoughts. For example, if we sit there and think "I want a drink of water," then we are distracted and our awareness becomes conditioned by that cause. But when we do not become distracted immediately and find ourselves in the presence of that moment, this is the measure of the stability of our practice. Also, when we are engaged in practice, there are various kinds of experiences in meditation (sgom nyams) which may arise through vision, sound, sensation, and so on. They arise spontaneously and are not conditioned by our conceptions or judgments. There may occur experiences of visions, such as lights, colors, auras, etc., or experiences of sensation, such as lightness of body, cessation of breathing, etc. These experiences (nyams) are merely manifestations of our elemental energies. There is nothing to fear in them. Since we have become relaxed, our energies are released and experiences of vision and sensation arise due to that fact.

(17) These experiences (nyams) not only arise in contemplation, but also after the session of practice is completed. Through developing our capacity for practice, we come to feel that everything is unreal, perceiving everything as being an illusion

(kun snang sgyu-mar mthong-ba). This represents a diminishing of our attachments. Or we may have an experience of emptiness; it seems as if this is actually occurring to us. This experience is very different from merely reading about Śūnyatā in a philosophy book or arriving at an understanding of Śūnyatā through an exhaustive intellectual analysis. Or we may develop a fear of the void. Or we may be capable of remaining in a state of pure presence and it seems that no thoughts arise. Or it may seem that we practitioners have developed to a level where we need not do any specific practice anymore, as if we could make no mistakes. Yet all of these are merely experiences in practice, and therefore they are not something bad or something which needs to be suppressed.

(18) If we want to observe the condition of the rays of the sun, the clouds which obscure the face of the sun must be removed first. Then the sun will be visible and the qualities of its self-perfectedness (lhun-grub) will begin to manifest themselves just as they are. This is what "attainment" (thob-pa) means; it is not a case of acquiring something which we do not already possess or of artificially producing or constructing something. The practitioner who finds himself in the state of pure presence does not simply remain at the level of a mere intellectual understanding of Śūnyatā, but he actually enters into the dimension of Śūnyatā. This is the attaining of the supreme Dharmakāya which is the Nature of Mind (sems-nyid chos kyi sku mchog thob-pa). The term *kāya* usually translated as "body," means one's entire dimension. Thus the Dharmakāya (chos-sku) is the dimension of all existence. Realizing this, whenever thoughts arise, they never become something concrete for us, but always remain in a condition of emptiness. Since we are no longer conditioned by thoughts and concepts, we attain the primal awareness of nondiscursiveness (rnam-par mi rtog-pa'i ye-shes thob-pa). By this means, one diminishes one's obstacles and obscurations.

(19) Since our obscurations (sgrib-pa) and our karmic traces (bag-chags) have been entirely purified, our passions (nyon-mongs) no longer manifest to disturb us. They are no longer out

of control (bag la nyal), jumping up at us like wild untamed horses. Even though we may be an ordinary person, living in the human dimension of flesh and blood, if we are capable of finding ourselves in the state of Rigpa, we have overcome the limitations of transmigration in Saṃsāra. This means we are no longer conditioned by what arises in the mind. A true practitioner of Dzogchen, finding himself in the state of Dzogchen, even though he is engaged in the concrete material world about him, is not conditioned by what surrounds him. Therefore, he does not suffer like an individual who takes everything about him to be solid, substantial, and real. We can say that such a person has overcome transmigration and karmic vision. Thus he or she belongs to the Family of the Āryas or Exalted Ones (the Arhats).

2. Relaxing with Presence

(20) The second consideration concerns the instructions for relaxing alertly with presence (lhug-pa'i man-ngag). The usual term for being relaxed is *glod-pa* or *lhod-pa.* However, we can be relaxed and yet be drowsy. The term *lhug-pa* means being relaxed, but alert and present. Thus, being alertly relaxed (lhug-pa), whenever appearances arise, in whatever fashion they may arise, then without the mind making any corrections or modifications of them, they are seen to exist as mere ornaments or embellishments of that state itself (rgyan gyi ngang-nyid) which is the real condition of existence (chos-nyid). In the Dzogchen Upadeśa, there is the practice of leaving vision just as it is (snang-ba'i co-bzhag). We do not enter into reasoning or into altering it with judgments. Thus, whenever appearances arise, they are left just as they are, and they in turn in no way condition the individual. These appearances (snang-ba) are like the ornaments (rgyan) of the individual's energy (rtsal). The individual finds himself in the true condition of the mirror. Anything which arises as an appearance is like the rising of a reflection in a mirror. These reflections, whether beautiful or ugly, in no way condition the mirror. Therefore, whatever arises creates no problems for the

individual. As the Master Phadampa said: "The individual is not conditioned by appearances but by his attachment to appearances; this attachment originates within the individual and not in the object." Internally, there exists a state of pure presence (rig-pa) which is uncorrected, clear, vivid, and naked (ma bcos sal hrig rjen-ne-ba). It is uncorrected and unmodified (ma bcos-pa) because it is unconditioned by discursive thoughts or the working of the mind. "Naked" (rjen-ne-ba) means that, in the instant when the thought arises, we are right there present and do not enter into any judgment or reasoning. Thus, while being alertly relaxed, when thoughts arise, we relax them into their own condition such as it is in itself (de-bzhin-nyid du rang sar glod-pa).

(21) "Relaxing with presence" means that when the senses have contact with an object, we do not enter into conceptualizing, reasoning or judging with respect to that object. Normally, when we see something, the mind makes a judgment with respect to it and as a reaction to this, a passion of attachment or aversion may arise. Then, by entering into action because of the passion, we come to accumulate more karma and so continue to transmigrate in Samsāra. However, the phrase "not entering into reasoning or analysis" (mi dpyod-pa) does not mean that we try to block thoughts. In Zen practice, for instance, one enters into a nondiscursive state (mi rtog-pa) where one experiences emptiness without any blocking of thoughts. For example, we may see a book on a table. We could take this book away or we could leave it where it is as if it were not something important. To block a thought means that we are taking something away and are trying to eliminate it. But when we speak of not entering into reasoning and judgment, this means leaving something just where it is, as it is, without being disturbed or distracted by it. Nonetheless, even though we do not enter into reasoning and judgment, thoughts continue to arise in a state of clearly aware presence without interruption or obstruction. It is important to understand what is meant by "not being distracted" (ma yengs) in the Dzogchen context. It means being aware. It does not mean that some mental

policeman keeps popping up inside the mind, saying "Now pay attention!"

When we find ourselves in a state of Rigpa, then its inherent qualities manifest as whatever appears, so that there is nothing to be interrupted or constructed. The sun's rays are the inherent nature of the sun when it shines. In the same way, everything arises as an ornament of one's energy, and this presence is self-perfected (lhun-grub) in this state. The idea of spontaneous self-perfection (lhun-grub) is a very important one in Dzogchen. If we were only to speak of primordial purity (ka-dag), then Dzogchen would be no different than Zen. But this understanding of *lhun-grub* sets Dzogchen apart from Zen. When we are present in the state of Rigpa, everything we see is a manifestation of our own individual energy (rtsal), like a reflection in a mirror. The whole dimension around oneself is spontaneously self-perfected in the potency of pure presence (rig-pa'i rtsal). As it says in the text: "When appearances, which are objects of the six sense faculties, arise as mere ornaments of one's state in a lucid fashion (sal-le-ba) without any obstruction ('gags-med) and without any analyses (mi dpyod), then they are entirely perfect and complete just as they are. They are experienced as the potency of pure presence (rig-pa'i rtsal) without any grasping or entering into conceptions and judgments ('dzin-med)." So we enter into this nondual state and continue in it present and relaxed. This is what is meant by *lhug-pa.*

(22) When we speak of a period of contemplation or *mnyam-bzhag,* this means being present in the state of Rigpa. The term *rjes-thob* refers to the time after the period of contemplation has been concluded. "Great Contemplation" (ting-'dzin chen-po) means that the practitioner has reached a level of development where his contemplation is no longer limited by formal periods of practice. But for the beginner, there are always these two moments of contemplation and non-contemplation. So, while continuing in the period of contemplation (mnyam-bzhag), without engaging in any analysis of or reasoning about (mi

dpyod-pa) the objects of the five gates of the senses, appearances are allowed to arise clearly and luminously in an alert, relaxed fashion without any distraction or grasping at conceptions and judgments (gsal dvangs mi g-yo 'dzin-med lhug-par shar). The term *mi g-yo-ba* means "unmoving" or "not distracted." When the state of Rigpa is interrupted, this is *g-yo-ba* or distraction. Śākyamuni Buddha is said to have been many times in a state of unmoving samādhi or undistracted concentration (mi g-yo-ba'i ting-nge-'dzin). But this did not mean that his physical body was necessarily immobile. Rather, it meant that He was in a state of pure presence (rig-pa) and He did not move from that, becoming distracted by mental activity. He was neither distracted nor conditioned by thoughts, and yet He performed all actions perfectly—moving and speaking and reasoning. Then, after this period of contemplation is concluded (rjes-thob), even when something concrete appears to the senses, it seems as if it has no inherent reality in itself. The case is the same with the passions; they have no inherent reality or self-nature. In this way, whatever arises to the senses becomes a means for remaining in primal awareness (ye-shes).

(23) Having considered external appearances (snang-ba), we now consider the subjective side of things, that is to say, the individual himself. The five poisons (dug lnga) are the five passions (nyon-mongs lnga) of delusion (gti-mug), anger (zhe-sdang), desire ('dod-chags), pride (nga-rgyal), and envy (phra-dogs). Whenever discursive thoughts (rnam-rtog) engendered by these five passions arise, we alertly relax (lhug-pa) in the face of them without entering into conceptions or judgments ('dzin-med). On the other hand, we should not try to block them by means of some antidote (gnyen-pos spang-ba) as we do in the Sūtra system or transform them by means of some method (thabs kyis bsgyur) as we do in the Tantra system. For example, in the Sūtra system the antidote to desire or attachment is meditation on the repulsiveness of the flesh, the antidote to anger is meditation on loving-kindness, the antidote to envy is rejoicing at the merit of others, and so on. And again, in the Tantra system, we

transform the passions into primal awareness, as for example, anger is transformed into the anger of a Heruka. Since they are neither blocked nor transformed, the passions which arise during the practice of the path are self-liberated (rang grol) and a primal awareness (ye-shes) is present.

When we are not in the state of Rigpa, the passions become poisons; since they interrupt and hinder our realization, they are called demons(bdud). They compel us to continue in transmigration. If we chase after a discursive thought and enter into mental activity, this thought may become a poison for us. In this way, we become a slave to our passions. But if we remain present, we will not be conditioned by our thoughts in any way and whatever arises will be merely like a reflection in a mirror. Thus, we need not apply some antidote to block the passion because the passion will self-liberate of itself. We are not even speaking here of *gcer-grol,* liberation through bare attention, that is to say, when we look into the face of a discursive thought which arises in the mind and it self-liberates. This procedure still involves some kind of effort. But this is not what we are speaking of here. The term *lhug-pa* means to relax with awareness. If we feel some passion arising, we then relax that passion without attempting to block it or trying to apply some antidote to it. We are not succumbing to the passion; it is simply that now the passion is governed by our awareness of presence (rig-pa). With this relaxed presence, our passions themselves become merely the inherent qualities of our primordial state manifesting themselves. This is the method for self-liberating the passions.

(24) Now we shall consider the experiences which arise during meditation practice (sgom nyams). Manifesting as clarity and emptiness (gsal zhing stong-par snang), they are found present in a state of vision and emptiness (snang la stong-pa'i ngang du gnas-pa) or in a state of the continuing movement of thoughts and emptiness ('gyu zhing stong), or in a state of pleasurable sensation and emptiness (bde la stong), etc. Thus, there may arise various different kinds of conscious experiences of the presence (shes nyams) of pleasurable sensation (bde-ba), of

clarity (gsal-ba), and of nondiscursiveness (mi rtog-pa). All of these experiences are linked to the individual.

(25) The term *kāya* means the entire dimension of our existence. Having understood all phenomena as the Dharmakāya, the entire dimension of existence (chos kun chos kyi skur rtogs te), we enter into a state of knowledge or awareness (shes-pa) of the real condition of things such as they are (de-bzhin-nyid kyi ngang) without any modifications made by the mind. This nondual self-perfected awareness is present like a perfect sphere (thig-le) which is whole, uniform, and without duality (gnyis-med mnyams rdzogs). Such a sphere has neither angles nor limits. And around this center, our energy manifests spontaneously self-perfected (lhun-grub). Thus, we may speak of attaining the whole Dimension of Primordial Awareness or the Jñānakāya (ye-shes sku) and a primal awareness of clarity (gsal-ba'i ye-shes) is present.

(26) Objects and their contact with the senses are many, but here the individual is no longer conditioned by these objects. Now we have a vivid experience: whatever arises has no inherent reality, but is like a reflection in a mirror. Since the objects which we perceive (gzung yul) are present as manifestations of the real condition of existence (chos-nyid snang-ba), our passions and obscurations become purified (nyon grib dag). In this way, we overcome the obstacle of the passions and are liberated. Because a primal awareness of pure presence (rig-pa'i ye-shes) is present within oneself, the individual can disentangle himself from engaging in negative behavior (tshul ngan bral). We are no longer limited by having to learn what to do and what not to do. We have overcome the limitations of the passions and have developed clarity. We are no longer slaves to external appearances, but govern ourselves autonomously with our own awareness. Negative attitudes and actions cannot arise. Why? Because all that arises in the individual which is negative arises through a lack of clarity and awareness. As the individual is liberated from his passions, karmic traces, and obscurations, he or she is now said to belong to the Family of the noble Bodhisattvas.

C. Progressing in the Practice

(27) We now come to consider the third topic: progressing in the practice (bogs dbyung); the previous two instructions concerned integrating (bsre-ba) and relaxing with presence (lhug-pa), both of which bring about stability in one's practice. Now, in order to benefit from and progress in this practice, from the very first instant our awareness must remain present and unmodified (skad-cig shes-pa ma bcos lhan-ner bzhag). It is a nondiscursive pure presence (mi rtog rig-pa) which is lucid and vivid (sal-le hrig-ge). The state of Rigpa is not conditioned by discursive thoughts. However, nondiscursiveness (mi rtog-pa) does not mean that discursive thoughts do not arise at all, only that we are not conditioned by their arising. Rigpa is spacious; there is always room for thoughts to arise. If this were not the case, then there would exist no way to integrate contemplation with daily life in terms of the activities of body, speech, and mind. However, the state of Rigpa is outside of and beyond time. Therefore, it is beyond the mind. We may find ourselves in a state of Rigpa and yet enter perfectly into all activities of body, speech, and mind. In the state of Rigpa it is possible for all kinds of thoughts to arise with no harm whatsoever, and moreover, there is the possibility of putting these thoughts into action. All that is required is that we must be clearly present in a state of presence. In this way, our continuity of awareness (shes rgyun) will remain stable and undistracted (ma yengs brtan-par skyang). This is how we progress in the practice.

(28) While continuing in the period of contemplation (mnyan-bzhag), one is neither influenced by drowsiness nor agitation, for in the genuine state of Rigpa there can be no defects. Moreover, everything manifests itself as emptiness which is the real condition of existence (chos-nyid stong-pa nyid du snang-ba). The whole of our vision arises as an ornament of the state of the individual. Since this is the case, there exists a way to reintegrate our energy. After the conclusion of a period of contemplation (rjes thob), without being conditioned by thoughts, we should

continue in the state of the Nature of Mind, which exists just as it is in itself (sems-nyid de-bzhin-nyid du skyang-bar bya).

(29) Then, with respect to experiences arising during meditation practice (sgom nyams), we find ourselves in a nondual state (gnyis-med ngang), whether we are meditating or not meditating. "Meditation" (sgom-pa) here does not mean a mental activity, such as visualization or analysis, but simply finding oneself in a state of presence (rig-pa). In this case, no conceptions or judgments, no mental limitations whatsoever, occur. Whatever appearances arise, whatever vision surrounds us, they will arise as an expression of the energy of the individual's contemplation (ting-'dzin rol-pa). The real condition of the existence of all phenomena just as they are (chos rnams kun kyi chos-nyid ji-bzhin-pa) presents itself without moving from the naturally occurring primordial situation (ye-babs gnas-lugs ngang las g-yo-med).

(30) In terms of our entire dimension (sku), whatever phenomena arise, whether visible or invisible, all of them are entirely purified by themselves in the state of the real condition of existence, the Dharmatā. "Purified" (yongs dag-pa) does not mean that we eliminate phenomena by some mental activity, but rather that the individual finds himself in their condition as it is and in this sense everything is "purified." There is no need to remove the reflections from the mirror. And indeed, the only way to get to the nature of the mirror is through the reflections. Here the individual finds himself in the actual capacity of the mirror to reflect, and so all these reflections are inherently pure. Thus, it is said that one attains the supreme dimension of nonduality (gnyis su med-pa'i sku mchog), where there is no longer a division between subject and object, and a primal awareness which is in no way clothed in mental activities (gos-pa med-pa'i ye-shes) is present.

(31) Through completely purifying our obscurations to knowledge (shes-bya'i sgrib-pa), and these may be very subtle indeed, we thus attain a knowledge of all phenomena as they are in the real condition of existence (chos-sku chos-nyid ji bzhin

mkhyen-pa). Since the individual is liberated from all dualistic considerations with respect to the one who knows and that which is known, he or she is said to belong to the Family of the omniscient Tathāgatas.

IV. The Practice of the Night

A. The Evening Practice

(32) Now, with respect to the practice of the night (mtshan-mo'i rnal-'byor), there are two practices: the first practice is done in the evening just before falling asleep; the second practice is done in the morning just when one awakens. When one is asleep, the senses are dormant. Therefore the individual must practice just before falling asleep, so that all his senses are present. We relax all the senses into a state of contemplation (mnyam-par bzhag-pa). We do not allow our senses to enter into a conditioned state; we just let things be as they are without becoming charged up in any way. Also, the individual must integrate his practice of concentration with his sleep (bsam-gtan gnyid dang bsre-bar bya). What does concentrated meditation or dhyāna (bsam-gtan) mean? When we fixate sharply with great attention on an object and then slowly relax our attention, the practice is called Śāmatha or Zhine (zhi-gnas), "calming the mind." When we work more with the movements of thoughts, this is called Vipaśyanā or Lhagthong (lhag-mthong). Dhyāna means meditating in this way. In this practice of the night there does exist at least a minimum of attention and holding one's mind in check. Then we must integrate this concentration with our sleep, so that we fall asleep with the presence of concentration.

(33) How do we do this? Just before falling asleep, visualize a white letter A ཨ or a small round bead (thig-le) of five-colored rainbow light in the space between our eyebrows. This is visualized clearly and is about the size of a pea. In the Dzogchen Upadeśa, this letter or a tiny sphere of white light is visualized in

the heart center because visualizing it between the eyebrows gives a sense of too much presence and one may not be able to fall asleep. But here we visualize it in the forehead center because this gives automatic control of all our vital energies or prāna (rlung). If it is difficult to visualize the white A here, adjustments should be made. The practitioner must proceed with awareness; the individual regulates the practice, not the practice the individual. It is of no use if we can do the visualization and then are not able to fall asleep. Nor should the visualization be overly brilliant, since this would inhibit falling asleep easily. The visualizing of a bindu (thig-le) or bead of multi-colored rainbow light, resembling a peacock's egg, is an alternative practice. If we should succeed in visualizing this five-colored bindu, this is very good for realizing control over the elements. First, we fixate (gtad-pa) our attention on this object of meditation, and then we relax (lhod-pa) our awareness a bit; otherwise, we will not be able to fall asleep.

(34) When we fall asleep in a state in which our six sense aggregates (tshogs drug) are alertly relaxed into their own condition (rang sar lhug-pa'i ngang-nyid du), our awareness will not become polluted by the grime of discursive thoughts (kun tu rtog-pa'i dri-mas ma sbags) and the natural Clear Light (rang-bzhin 'od-gsal) appears. When we are concentrating or fixating on a single object of meditation, there is no room for extraneous thoughts to arise. But when we relax a bit, it is easy for them to rise and for the individual to become conditioned by them. We should not try to block these thoughts, but if we are not sufficiently present, we will become distracted. We will then get caught up in these thoughts and sleep will not come right away. But if we continue in the presence of a relaxed state, sleep will come easily. This means that we have integrated this pure presence (rig-pa) with sleep and this is called the natural Clear Light (rang-bzhin 'od gsal). Then we will find ourselves in the presence of the real condition of existence, the Dharmatā (chos-nyid ngang du gnas), undistracted by discursive thoughts.

(35) However, if we are able to do the visualization and yet cannot fall asleep, what is there to do then? When we go to bed,

thoughts continue to arise because the mind continues to function. So when a thought arises, at that instant of awareness (skad-cig shes-pa), we find ourselves present with bare awareness with respect to whatever arises. We continue in this limpidly clear presence (rig-pa), even if other thoughts intrude. But we do not see anything whatsoever in them which can be identified as the calm state or the movement of thought (gnas 'gyu'i rang-ngo gang yang mthong med). This procedure will in no way impede the individual from falling asleep. But if we charge up the mind by thinking and getting caught up in many different things through distraction, then we will not be able to fall asleep. However, a state of presence (rig-pa) will in no way damage our sleep. Thus, finding ourselves in a state of alert vibrant presence (seng-nge-ba), we settle into a quiet awareness (shes pa tsan-ner bzhag) and fall asleep.

(36) The process of falling asleep (gnyid log) is itself the cause of our being able to enter into the clarity of the real condition of existence (chos nyid gsal-ba'i rkyen). The functioning of all our senses, in a state of presence, finds itself absorbed entirely into the Dharmadhātu (chos-dbyings ngang la yongs thim). Until we have fallen asleep entirely, we can find ourselves present in that state of contemplation.

(37) When we fall asleep, we become disengaged from the karmic traces of the material body (lus kyi bag-chags), the karmic traces of vision (snang-ba'i bag-chags), and the karmic traces of mental functioning (yid kyi bag-chags). These karmic traces, during the waking state, manifest as our material body, the external appearances which we perceive, and the functioning of our minds, respectively. Why do we speak of being disengaged? For example, the solid walls of a room present material limitations. We cannot pass freely through them. But when we are present in the state of Rigpa, then we are not conditioned by the material body. When we are present in this state, there is a way to overcome these limitations and we find ourselves in the real condition of existence. How is this? From one's falling asleep right up to the moment when we begin to dream, there is no

functioning of the mind (yid mi 'byung) and we find ourselves in the presence of the real condition of existence (chos-nyid ngang gnas-pa). In this, we will experience to a certain degree a merging with what is called the natural Clear Light (rang-bzhin 'od-gsal 'dres-pa'i tshad du shes). This being the case, we will be able with no further effort to experience lucid dreams and control their contents. Moreover, at the moment of death, we will be able to die with complete presence and awareness. And when we die with presence, then in the Chonyid Bardo (chos nyid bar-do) all the apparitions which appear will simply arise as the manifestation of spontaneous self-perfection (lhun-grub) and we will recognize them as such. These spontaneously self-perfected qualities which appear are those of the Sambhogakāya. Falling asleep is an analogous process to dying, and so attaining mastery over the dream state in this life will allow us to realize mastery over death and the Bardo state. Falling asleep in a state of the natural Clear Light is equivalent to the experience of the Chonyid Bardo.

The next phase is the onset of dreaming. The dream state is analogous to the Sidpa Bardo (srid-pa'i bar-do). The latter is called "the Bardo of Becoming" because it represents the onset of the rebirth process. When we are aware that we have found ourself in the Bardo, there are many things which we can do to better our situation. As in the case with the dream state, in the Bardo we are not conditioned by a material body, and yet all the sense faculties function. Thus, a practitioner, because of his practice during his lifetime, will be in a much better position and will have developed far greater clarity than the ordinary individual who finds himself in the after-death experience. Because of his greater clarity, in the Bardo the practitioner will have the capacity to understand his condition and what is happening. He will not be helplessly and blindly driven hither and yon by the winds of his karma. But this capacity will only come about if one is aware and present while in the Bardo. This is analogous to lucid dreaming and so we can use the dream state to realize this capacity in daily practice. In the waking state, we can only go out of a room by way of the door, but in the dream state, we can pass through seemingly solid walls. This experience of the dream state is very favorable for the overcoming of attachments in daily life, because we experience directly the insubstantiality and unreality of everything.

(38) When we find ourselves in the state of the natural Clear Light, discursive thoughts which create distractions do not arise. Our state of presence is absorbed into its Mother (rig-pa mar thim) which is the natural Clear Light and we find ourselves present in the state of the Dharmatā, the real condition of existence (chos-nyid ngang du gnas). It is like an only son meeting his mother after a long separation. Thus we speak of the "Son Clear Light" which is experienced in practice during one's lifetime and the "Mother Clear Light" which is experienced here upon falling asleep, and more especially, at the moment of death. What we are looking at here is the principle of the reintegration of energy. As the result of the natural Clear Light practice, in the period subsequent to contemplation (rjes thob), and in this case, it is the dream state which is meant, we begin to experience awareness in dreams, recognizing dreams to be dreams while we are still sleeping. Therefore, with the practice of the natural Clear Light, we do not need any other special dream practice or yoga. And finding ourselves freed of all illusions and delusions ('khrul bral), dreams will arise as helpful friends to manifesting our entire dimension of existence and its primordial awareness (sku dang ye-shes grogs su shar).

There are two ways to look at this overcoming of illusions ('khrul-pa). First, through recognizing dreams to be dreams while we are yet asleep, we become aware of the illusory nature of the dream state, and during the waking state, we become more conscious of the illusory nature of everything in daily life. Second, we are no longer the slave of dreams and sleep. While sleeping, we tend to be conditioned by dreams through the same factors that condition us in daily life. So, by means of this practice dreaming becomes a way to discover true knowledge and this becomes a way to develop the manifestation of our Dimension and our Primordial Awareness (sku dang ye-shes). This sums up the evening practice.

B. The Morning Practice

(39) But there is also a practice for the morning when we are awakening from sleep. What do we do here? When we awaken in the early morning, a primal awareness arises which is uncorrected by the mind and which is present in its own condition (ye-shes rang-so ma bcos-pa). Then we usually enter again into the functioning of our mind and senses, just like a dead person finding himself reborn into a new body. However, if, on the other hand, we remain in this natural state of pure presence without any distraction and without any constructed meditation (sgom med yengs med rnal-mar bzhag-pa), then we will find ourselves quietly present in our own inherent nature, undisturbed by any discursive thoughts (rang-bzhin mi rtog lhan-ner gnas-pa). An individual who finds himself in that state cannot be conditioned by any external appearances or by discursive thoughts. This is known as the state (dgongs-pa) of the supreme Guru Samantabhadra. Samantabhadra (kun-tu bzang-po) represents the true primordial state of the individual, his "Secret Guru" (gsang-ba'i bla-ma), so to speak. Here also is a way to practice an essential Guru Yoga. We must understand that this very state of Rigpa is identical with the state of the Guru or Master himself, and that this state of Rigpa is none other than our own innate primordial state. Therefore, Guru Yoga is not a matter of uniting or merging two separate entities, the Master and oneself; rather, from the very beginning, they have been inseparable. Experiencing the recognition of the inseparability of the state of the Master and our own state is the way to practice the supreme Guru Yoga.

(40) Thus, when we awaken, finding ourselves in a state of presence, we look with a bare attention (gcer gyis bltas-pa) into the face of that very state of presence (rang ngor bltas) to see what may be there. However, in this moment of being present, we do not find anything at all recognizable or confirmable (ngos bzung

bral-ba). Moreover, we do not find any meditator, that is, any one who is meditating (sgom-mkhan). Thus, this lucid and naked self-originated primal awareness, which arises upon awakening and which does not find anything confirmable, self-liberates as it arises (rang-byung ye-shes sal-le rjen-ne-ba shar grol). Thereby, a nondual primal awareness (gnyis-med ye-shes) becomes present. This is a very important point in practice. Although we may be speaking here of awaking in the morning, in fact we should try to do this practice at every moment. The reason for this is that even if we believe that we are very present in a state of awareness (rig-pa), still a kind of drowsiness or sleepiness may remain. To deal with this, we should not resort to some kind of strategy, thinking that first we must do this and then do that. Rather, just in being present there is found an antecedent condition which is directing us toward a state of Rigpa. However, this condition does not involve any thinking, any working of the mind, but is simply a way of finding ourselves in a state of presence in which there is increasing clarity. This is also a way to "refresh" our contemplation in general, and is referred to by that famous term "self-originated primal awareness" (rang byung ye-shes).

(41) Thus, upon awakening in the morning, a nondual primal awareness arises, and as it arises, it liberates itself by itself. At that moment, finding ourselves beyond our usual karmic vision of an objective world (snang yul bral) and transcending all dualistic thoughts (gnyis 'dzin kun rtog las 'das), a primal awareness of nondiscursiveness (mi rtog ye-shes) becomes clearly manifest. Thus, we remain present in this awareness which is in no way conditioned by discursive thoughts. Since we are present in awareness in this way, a primal awareness of clarity, unsullied by the taint of discursive thoughts (ma bslad gsal-ba'i ye-shes), becomes clearly manifest. And since we do not remain at the dualistic level of subject and object, a primal awareness of pleasurable sensation (bde-ba'i ye-shes) becomes clearly manifest.

(42) Thereupon, there arises a supreme primal awareness which is in no way mistaken (gol-ba med-pa'i ye-shes) because we have understood that all phenomena are in themselves the real

condition of existence (chos kun chos-nyid rang du rtogs 'gyur). Then, since a primal awareness of quantity (ji snyed ye-shes) which knows each thing in its individuality, becomes clearly manifest in its entirety, the inherent nature of the Trikāya, or the three dimensions of our existence (sku gsum), becomes supremely manifest.

V. The Benefits of the Practice

(43) When we practice in this way both day and night, the whole of the dimension of our life enters into contemplation (ting-'dzin khor-yug chen-po). Slowly the individual's degree of capacity develops, so that he becomes familiar with this. Thereupon, our passions will arise as something useful on the path. And moreover, we will develop a certain measure of capacity to help others by way of the Trikāya, the three dimensions of one's existence.

(44) The degree to which we become familiar ('byongs tshad) with the practice can be measured by the extent of our control over the dream state, recognizing our dreams to be dreams while still sleeping (rmi-lam gnyid du ngo-shes). Through practice, day by day we overcome attachments and so sensations of pleasure and pain no longer condition the individual. And we find ourselves in a state of integration which is in no way clothed in conceptions and judgments (ma-gos mnyam-nyid ngang). Because primal awareness is present, all appearances arise as friends (kun snang grogs su shar) who can help one on the path. In fact, everything encountered along the path can now be something utilized to help develop our practice. Therefore, we can interrupt the continuity of illusory vision ('khrul-pa'i rgyun chad) and we find ourselves in the state of the Dharmatā, the real condition of existence.

(45) The accomplished practitioner of Dzogchen finds himself in the state of the real condition of existence (chos-nyid

ngang) and remains there without moving from it both day and night. "Unmoving" (ma g-yos) means stability in this state of presence. Thus, Buddhahood ('tshang-rgya) may be realized even in the instant between two breaths.

(46) How can the passions be utilized when they arise on the path? Without categorizing phenomena (chos kun dbyer med) as either good or bad, we find them present in the state of the real condition of existence (chos-nyid ngang gnas). This is what is usually meant by *ro-gcig,* "of a single taste." Because all of them are present in total awareness without there being any conceptualization with regard to them (kun rig dmigs-med), we recognize the passion of delusion (gti-mug) itself as being nothing other than nondiscursiveness (mi rtog-par ngo-shes-pa). In other words, while we are in a state of pure presence (rig-pa), when the passion of delusion arises, we find ourselves in a state of nondiscursiveness (mi rtog-pa). All phenomena manifest as the real condition of existence just as it is in itself (chos-nyid de-bzhin-nyid du snang-ba). Emptiness and spontaneous self-perfection are both present simultaneously in this primal awareness.

(47) All phenomena which present themselves as objects to the six sense aggregates (tshogs drug yul du snang-ba'i chos rnams) are present in luminous clarity (gsal-ba) and lacking in any inherent nature (rang-bzhin med). Although lacking in any inherent nature, they are present as the real condition of existence. At the moment when it arises, we recognize the passion of anger (zhe-sdang) to have the character of clarity (gsal-ba'i rang-bzhin ngo-shes) and this passion manifests as the primal awareness of clarity (gsal-ba ye-shes nyid du snang-ba).

(48) Everything which appears externally (phyir snang), all of our external vision, is none other than the state of the real condition of existence (chos-nyid), while internally the state of pure presence (nang rig) is itself primal awareness (ye-shes). However, we should not think that these two (the Dharmatā and Rigpa) are ultimately distinct and separate. If such were the case, integration would not be possible. But we do not remain at this

level of distinguishing external as against internal. This realization of their inseparability gives rise to a manifestation of great bliss of Mahāsukha, which is nondual in nature (gnyis-med bde-chen). And because it has the nature of Energy or compassion (thugs-rje'i bdag-nyid), the passion of desire ('dod-chags) is recognized to be in actuality the potency of great bliss (bde-chen rtsal du ngo-shes). And thus there manifests a primal awareness of the sensation of great bliss which is spontaneously self-perfected without any limitations (lhun 'byams bde-chen ye-shes snang-ba). This is how the passions can be utilized on the path.

(49) The capacity to benefit all other beings ('gro kun) is realized by way of developing the three dimensions of one's existence. The individual has three levels of existence in terms of the functioning of his body, speech (or energy), and mind. When we fully realize ourselves, there are various ways in which this realization can manifest, and this represents the manifestation of the Trikāya or the three dimensions of our existence (sku gsum). The term Nirmāṇakāya indicates one's material dimension or body, the term Sambhogakāya indicates the subtle dimension of one's energy, and the term Dharmakāya indicates the Dimension of Existence and its inherent Primordial Awareness (sku dang ye-shes). Here the three poisonous passions (nyon-mongs dug gsum) are no longer called poisons; but because the individual has attained realization, these very same poisons manifest themselves entirely as one's Dimension of Existence and one's inherent Primordial Awareness (sku dang ye-shes su yongs su snang-ba). And because of that, whatever arises from them is also present in one's whole Dimension of Existence as its inherent infinite Primordial Awareness (sku dang ye-shes nyid du gnas).

(50) Since there no longer exist any passions as such and since the causes of the passions have been entirely eliminated, one has transcended transmigrating in Saṃāra. One has arrived at that condition which is called Nirvāṇa (myang-'das), which literally means "having gone beyond suffering." But, even though it is given the name Nirvāṇa, as if one has arrived somewhere or attained something, in truth there has been no arrival and

nothing attained. Rather, it is simply that the inherent qualities of the state of the individual have spontaneously manifested themselves as self-perfected without any corrections or modifications made by mind (ma bcos lhun-grub ji snyed yon-tan tshogs). Nothing has to be changed, corrected, or modified; everything is perfect just as it is in being the spontaneous manifestation of the primordial state of the individual. It is simply the case that what was inherent from the very beginning has now manifested, just as the sun appears in the sky when the clouds dissipate. This is what is meant by "clarity" (gsal-ba).

VI. Qualities of the Practitioner

(51) In the supreme vehicle of Dzogchen Atiyoga, it is said that this practice is well adapted to the practitioner who possesses five capacities: 1. willingness to participate or faith (dad-pa); 2. diligence in practice (brtson-'grus); 3. presence or mindfulness (dran-pa); 4. concentration (ting-nge'dzin); and 5. intelligence or wisdom (shes-rab). We need all of these five capacities. Being wise and acting in an intelligent fashion, we should set about to realize the harmonious conditions (mthun rkyen) for cultivating such capacity when it is lacking or needed. Thus one will not lose the supreme opportunity to practice Dzogchen.

VII. Conclusion

(52) When we do something according to the Mahāyāna Sūtra system, the altruistic intention to benefit others must be present. Moreover, the understanding of emptiness and of the illusory nature of everything must not be lacking. Then, at the conclusion, one must dedicate any merit accumulated by the action to the benefit of other beings. Here, a little of the essential nectar of the teaching of the Master Garab Dorje has been presented with the

wish that all who will have contact with it will come to realize for themselves the state of Samantabhadra (kun-bzang dgongs-pa), the primordial state of the individual.

Biographical Sketch of the Author

The author of this text on rDzogs chen practice, Nam mkha'i Norbu Rinpoche, was born in the village of dGe'ug, in the lCong ra district of sDe dge in East Tibet, on the eighth day of the tenth month of the Earth-Tiger year (1938). His father was sGrol ma Tshe ring, member of a noble family and sometime official with the government of sDe dge, and his mother was Ye shes Chos sgron.

When he was two years old, he was recognized by both dPal yul Karma Yang srid Rinpoche[1] and Zhe chen Rab byams Rinpoche[2] as the reincarnation of A'dzom 'Brug pa.[3] A 'dzom 'Brug pa was one of the great rDzogs chen Masters of the early part of this century. He was the disciple of the first mKhyen brtse Rinpoche, 'Jam dbyangs mKhyen brtse dBang po (1829-1892), and also the disciple of dPal sprul Rinpoche.[4] Both of these illustrious teachers were leaders of the *Ris med* or non-sectarian movement in nineteenth-century eastern Tibet. On some thirty-seven occasions, A'dzom 'Brug pa received transmissions from his principal master, 'Jam dbyangs mKhyen brtse, and from dPal sprul Rinpoche he received the complete transmissions of the *kLong chen snying thig* and the *rTsa rlung* precepts. In turn, A'dzom 'Brug pa became a *gter ston,* or discoverer of hidden treasure texts, having received visions directly from the incomparable 'Jigs med gLing pa (1730-1798) when the former was thirty. Teaching at A'dzom sgar in eastern Tibet during summer and winter retreats,[5] A'dzom 'Brug pa became the master of many contemporary teachers of rDzogs chen. Among them was Norbu Rinpoche's paternal uncle, rTogs ldan O rgyan bsTan 'dzin,[6] who was his first rDzogs chen teacher.

When he was eight years old, Norbu Rinpoche was recognized by both the sixteenth Karmapa[7] and dPal spung Situ Rinpoche[8] to be the mind-incarnation[9] of Lho 'Brug Zhabs drung Rinpoche.[10] This latter master, the reincarnation of the illustrious 'Brug pa bKa' brgyud master, Padma dKar po (1527-1592), was the actual historical founder of the state of Bhutan. Until the early twentieth century, the Zhabs drung Rinpoches were the Dharmarajas or temporal and spiritual rulers of Bhutan.

While yet a child, from rDzogs chen mKhan Rinpoche,[11] from his maternal uncle mKhyen brtse Yang srid Rinpoche,[12] and from his paternal uncle rTogs ldan O rgyan bsTan 'dzin, Norbu Rinpoche received instruction in the *rDzogs chen gsang ba snying thig* and the *sNying thig Yab bzhi.* Meanwhile, from gNas rgyab mChog sprul Rinpoche,[13] he received the transmissions of the *rNying ma bka' ma,* the *kLong gsal rdo rje snying po,* and the *gNam chos* of Mi 'gyur rDo rje. From mKhan Rinpoche dPal ldan Tshul khrims (1906-) he received the transmissions from the *rGyud sde kun btus,* the famous Sa skya pa collection of tantric practices. And in addition, he received many initiations and listened to many oral explanations[14] from famous Ris med pa or nonsectarian masters of eastern Tibet.

From the time he was eight years old until he was twelve, he attended the college of sDe dge dbon stod slob grwa at sDe dge dgon chen Monastery, where, with mKhen Rinpoche mKhyen rab Chos kyi 'od zer (1901-), he studied the thirteen basic texts[15] used in the standard academic curriculum designed by mKhan po gZhan dga'.[16] Norbu Rinpoche became especially expert in the *Abhisamayālaṅkāra.* In addition, with this same master he studied the great commentary to the *Kālacakra Tantra,*[17] the *Guhyagarbha Tantra,* the *Zab mo nang don* of Karmapa Rang byung rDo rje, the Medical Tantras,[18] Indian and Chinese astrology,[19] as well as receiving from him the initiations and transmissions of the *Sa skya'i sgrub thabs kun btus.*

From the age of eight until he was fourteen, at the college of sDe dge Ku se gSer ljongs bshad grwa, from mKhan Rinpoche Brag gyab Blos gros (1913-), he received instructions in the *Prajñāpāramitā Sūtras,* the *Abhisamayālaṅkāra,* and three tantric texts: the *rDorje Gur,* the *Hevajra Tantra,* and the *Saṃputa Tantra.*[20] By his tutor mChog sprul Rinpoche[21] he was instructed in the secular sciences.[22]

Also, from the age of eight until he was fourteen, having gone to rDzong gsar Monastery in eastern Tibet, he received teachings from the illustrious rDzong gsar mKhyen brtse Rinpoche[23] on the *Sa skya'i zab chos lam 'bras,* the quintessential doctrine of the Sa skya pa school and, in addition, on the three texts: *rGyud kyi spyi don rnam bzhag, lJon shing chen mo,* and the *Hevajra Tantra.*[24] Then at the college of Khams bre bshad grwa, with mKhan Rinpoche Mi nyag Dam chos (1920-) he studied a basic text on logic, the *Tshad ma rig gter* of Sa skya Paṇḍita.

Then, in the meditation cave at Seng-chen gNam brag, he made a retreat with his uncle the rTogs ldan O rgyan bsTan 'dzin for the practices of Vajrapāṇi, Siṃhamukha, and White Tārā. At that time, the son of A'dzom 'Brug pa, 'Gyur med rDo rje (1895-), returned from Central Tibet, and staying with them, the latter bestowed the cycle of *rDo rje gro lod,* the *Klong chen snying thig,* and the cycle of the *dGongs pa zang thal* of Rig 'dzin rGod ldem 'Phru can.

When he was fourteen years old in 1951, he received the initiations for Vajrayogini according to the Ngor pa and Tshar pa traditions of the Sa skya. Then his tutor advised him to seek out a woman living in the Kadari region who was the living embodiment of Vajrayogini herself and take initiation from her. This woman master, A yo mKha' 'gro rDo rje dPal sgron (1838-1953), was a direct disciple of the great 'Jam dbyangs mKhyen brtse dBang po and of Nyag bla Padma bDud 'dul, as well as being an elder contemporary of A 'dzom 'Brug pa. At this time she was one hundred and thirteen years old and had been in a dark retreat[25] for some fifty-six years. Norbu Rinpoche received from her transmissions for the *mKha' 'gro gsang 'dus,* the mind-treasure[26] of 'Jam dbyangs mKhyen brtse dBang po, and the *mKha' 'gro yang thig,* in which the principal practice is the dark retreat, as well as the *kLong chen snying thig.* She also bestowed upon him her own mind-treasures, including that for the Dākinī Siṃhamukha, the *mKha' 'gro dbang mo'i seng ge gdong ma'i zab thig.*

Then in 1954, he was invited to visit the People's Republic of China as a representative of Tibetan youth. From 1954 he was an instructor in Tibetan language at the Southwestern University of Minor Nationalities at Chengdu, Sichuan, China. While living in China, he met the famous Gangs dkar Rinpoche.[27] From the master he heard many explanations of the Six Doctrines of Nāropa,[28] Mahāmudrā, the *dKon mchog spyi 'dus,* as well as Tibetan medicine. During this time, Norbu Rinpoche also acquired proficiency in the Chinese and Mongolian languages.

When he was seventeen years old, returning to his home country of sDe dge following a vision received in dream, he came to meet his Root Master,[29] Nyag bla Rinpoche Rig 'dzin Byang chub rDo rje (1826-1978), who lived in a remote valley to the east of sDe gde. Byang chub rDo rje Rinpoche hailed originally from the Nyag rong region on the borders of China. He was a disciple of A 'dzom 'Brug pa, of Nyag bla Padma bDud 'dul, and of Shar rdza Rinpoche,[30] the famous Bonpo teacher of rDzogs chen who attained the Rainbow Body of Light.[31] A practicing physician, Byang chub rDo rje Rinpoche headed a commune called Nyag bla sGar in this remote valley; it was a totally self-supporting community consisting entirely of lay practitioners, yogins and yoginis. From this master, Norbu Rinpoche received initiation into, and transmission of, the essential teachings of rDzogs chen *Sems sde, Klong sde,* and *Man ngag gi sde.* More importantly, this master introduced him directly to the experience of rDzogs chen. He remained here for almost a year, often assisting Byang chub rDo rje Rinpoche in his medical practice and serving as his scribe and secretary. He also received transmissions from the master's son, Nyag sras 'Gyur med rDo rje.

After this, Norbu Rinpoche set out on a prolonged pilgrimage to Central Tibet, Nepal, India, and Bhutan. Returning to sDe dge, the land of his birth, he found that deteriorating political conditions had led to the eruption of violence. Travelling on first toward Central Tibet, he finally emerged safely in Sikkim. From 1958 to 1960 he lived in Gangtok, Sikkim, employed as an author and editor of Tibetan text books for the Development Office, the Government of Sikkim. In 1960, when he was twenty-two years old, at the invitation of Professor Giuseppe Tucci, he went to Italy and resided for several years in Rome. During this time, from 1960 to 1964, he was a research associate at the Istituto Italiano per il Medio ed Estremo Oriente. Receiving a grant from the Rockefeller Foundation, he worked in close collaboration with Professor Tucci, and wrote two appendices to Professor Tucci's *Tibetan Folk Songs of Gyantse and Western Tibet* (Rome, 1966), as well as giving seminars at IsMEO on yoga, medicine, and astrology.

From 1964 to the present, Norbu Rinpoche has been a professor at the Istituto Orientale, University of Naples, where he teaches Tibetan language, Mongolian language, and Tibetan cultural history. Since then he has done extensive research into the historical origins of Tibetan culture, investigating little-known literary sources from the Bonpo tradition. In 1983, Norbu Rinpoche hosted the first International Convention on Tibetan Medicine held in Venice, Italy. Although still actively teaching at the university, for the past ten years Norbu Rinpoche has informally conducted teaching retreats in various countries, including Italy, France, England, Austria, Denmark, Norway, Finland, and since 1979, the United States. During these retreats, he gives practical instruction in rDzogs chen practices in a non-sectarian format, as well as teaching aspects of Tibetan culture, especially Yantra Yoga, Tibetan medicine, and astrology. Moreover, under his guidance there has grown up, at first in Italy and now in several other countries, including the United States, what has come to be known as the Dzogchen Community.[32] This is an informal association of individuals who, while continuing to work at their usual occupations in society, share a common interest in pursuing and practicing the teachings which Norbu Rinpoche continues to transmit.

The above information was largely extracted by John Reynolds from a biography in Tibetan appended to Professor Norbu's *gZi yi Phreng ba* (Dharamsala: Library of Tibetan Works and Archives, 1982).

Notes to the Biography

1. Kun-bzang 'gro 'dul 'od gsal klong yangs rdo rje, 1898- .
2. sNang mdzod grub pa'i rdo rje, 1900- .
3. 'Gro 'dul dpa' bo rdo rje, 1842-1924.
4. rDza dPal sprul Rin po che, O rgyan 'jigs med chos kyi dbang po, 1808-87.
5. During summer retreats he taught rDzogs chen and during winter retreats he taught *rtsa rlung,* the yoga of the channels and energies.
6. The term *rtogs ldan* means "one who has attained understanding," and is more or less synonymous with *rnal 'byor pa,* "a yogin."
7. rGyal ba Karmapa, Rang 'byung rig pa'i rdo rje, 1924-81.
8. Padma dbang mchog rgyal po, 1886-1952.
9. thugs kyi sprul sku.
10. Ngag dbang rnam rgyal, 1594-1651.
11. Kun dga' dpal ldan, 1878-1950.
12. 'Jam dbyangs chos kyi dbang phyug, 1910-73.
13. 'Jam dbyangs blo gros rgya mtsho, 1902-52.
14. dbang dang khrid.
15. *gzhung chen bcu gsum.* These texts are:
    1. *Prātimokṣa Sūtra*
    2. *Vinaya Sūtra* by Gunaprabha
    3. *Abhidharmasamuccaya* by Asaṅga
    4. *Abhidharmakoṣa* by Vasubandhu
    5. *Mūlamadhyamakakārikā* by Nāgārjuna
    6. *Madhyamakāvatāra* by Candrakīrti
    7. *Catuḥśatakā* by Āryadeva
    8. *Bodhicaryāvatāra* by Śāntideva
    9. *Abhisamayālaṅkāra* by Maitreya/Asanga
    10. *Mahāyānasūtrālaṅkāra* by Maitreya/Asanga

11. *Madhyāntavibhaṅga* by Maitreya/Asanga
12. *Dharmadharmatāvibhaṅga* by Maitreya/Asanga
13. *Uttaratantra* by Maitreya/Asanga

16. gZhan phan chos kyi snang ba.
17. Dus 'khor 'grel chen.
18. *rGyud bzhi.*
19. *rtsis dkar nag.*
20. *gur brtag sam gsum.*
21. Yongs 'dzin mchog sprul, Kun dga' grags pa, 1922- .
22. *rig gnas kyi skor.*
23. rDzong gsar mkhyen brtse Rin po che, Jam mgon mkhyen sprul Chos kyi blo gros, 1896-1959.
24. *spyi ljon brtag gsum.* The *Hevajra Tantra* is also known as the *brtag gnyis* because it is divided into two parts.
25. *mun mtshams.*
26. *dgongs gter.*
27. Gangs dkar Rin po che, Karma bshad sprul Chos kyi seng ge, 1903-56.
28. Na ro chos drug.
29. rtsa ba'i bla ma.
30. Shar rdza bKra shis rgyal mtshan, 1859-1935.
31. *'ja' lus pa.*
32. *rdzogs chen 'dus sde.*

Books by Namkhai Norbu

1. *Manuale di lingua tibetana* (Naples: Comunità Dzogchen, 1977): an introductory grammar and reader of Tibetan language (in Italian).
2. *Zhang Bod Lo rgyus* (Naples: Comunità Dzogchen, 1981): a collection of texts dealing with the ancient history of Zhang Zhung and Tibet (in Tibetan and Italian).
3. *Bod kyi lo rgyus las 'phros pa'i gtam nor bu'i do shal* (Dharamsala: Library of Tibetan Works and Archives, 1981): a new interpretation of ancient Tibetan history and culture (in Tibetan).
4. *The Necklace of gZi: A Cultural History of Tibet* (Dharamsala: Library of Tibetan Works and Archives, 1981): an investigation of the origins of Tibetan culture in the ancient civilization of Zhang Zhung.
5. *gZi yi phreng ba* (Dharamsala: Library of Tibetan Works and Archives, 1982): Tibetan text of the above.
6. *Yantra Yoga* (Naples: Comunità Dzogchen, 1982): a treatise on the classical system of Yantra Yoga of Vairocana (in Tibetan).
7. *Byang 'brog lam yig* (Arcidosso: Shang Shung Edizioni, 1983): an account of the culture of the nomadic tribes of North Tibet (in Tibetan).
8. *On Birth and Life: A Treatise on Tibetan Medicine* (Venice: Shang Shung Edizioni, 1983): a summary of Tibetan medicine.

9. *The Mirror: Advice on Presence and Awareness* (Arcidosso: Shang Shung Edizioni, 1983): an introduction to Dzogchen practice.
10. *Primordial Experience: Mañjuśrīmitra's Treatise on the Meaning of Bodhicitta in rDzogs chen*, with K. Lipman, in collaboration with B. Simmons (Boston: Shambhala, 1987).
11. *The Small Collection of Hidden Precepts: A Study of An Ancient Manuscript on Dzogchen from Tun-huang* (Arcidosso: Shang Shung Edizioni, 1984): a study of Buddhagupta's *sBa pa'i rGum chung* (in Tibetan).
12. *The Crystal and the Way of Light: Sutra, Tantra and Dzogchen*, compiled and edited by John Shane (London and New York: Routledge ț Kegan Paul, 1986): a systematic presentation of the teachings of Namkhai Norbu.
13. *Dzogchen: The Self-Perfected State*, edited by Adriano Clemente and translated into English by John Shane. (Publication in English forthcoming, translated from an original book in Italian published by Ubaldini Editore, 1986, with the title *Dzogchen: lo stato di autoperfecione.)*

About the Translator

John Myrdhin Reynolds studied Comparative Religion, Anthropology, Sanskrit, Tibetan, and Buddhist Philosophy at Columbia University, the University of California at Berkeley, and the University of Washington. He did his principal work in Sanskrit and Buddhist Philosopy under Dr. Edward Conze. He then spent eight years in India and Nepal researching and practicing Tantra Yoga and meditation under various prominent Tibetan Lamas and Hindu Yogins. He was initiated into both the Nyingmapa and Kagyudpa orders of Tibetan Buddhism and subsequently received ordination in Darjeeling as a Tantric Buddhist Yogin under the name of Vajranātha. He has lectured widely in India, Europe, and America and has taught Comparative Religion and Buddhist Studies at Shanti Ashram (South India), the University of Massachusetts (Amherst), U.C. Santa Cruz, and most recently at the College of New Rochelle in New York. He has published both in Nepal and the West a number of books and articles on Tantra, Buddhist psychology and meditation, and Tibetan astrology, as well as translations from Tibetan texts. He has collaborated with Prof. Namkhai Norbu on a number of translation projects and now lives in Devon, England. His translation, with extensive commentary, of *Self-Liberation Through Seeing Everything in its Nakedness: An Introduction to the Nature of One's Own Mind*, foreword by Namkhai Norbu, is also being published by Station Hill Press.

Glossary of Technical Terms

English-Tibetan

after a period of contemplation	rjes thob
analysis, analyze	dpyod pa
appearance, to appear	snang ba
awareness	shes pa
clarity, clear	gsal ba
contemplation	ting nge 'dzin (*samādhi*)
concentration	bsam gtan (*dhyāna*)
conception, imagination	dmigs pa
continuity of awareness	shes rgyun
dimension of existence	sku (*kāya*)
discursive thought	rnam rtog
drowsiness and agitation	bying rgod
Energy	thugs rje
essence	ngo bo
experience after meditating	rjes nyams
experiences during meditation	sgom nyams
experience of clarity	gsal ba'i nyams
experience of non-discursiveness, emptiness	mi rtog pa'i nyams
experience of pleasurable sensation	bde ba'i nyams
free of illusion	'khrul bral
Great Perfection	rdzogs chen
integrate, mix	bsre ba
integrate into space	nam mkha' ar gtad
intelligence	shes rab
intention, state	dgongs pa
just as it is	de bzhin nyid
karmic traces	bag chags
karmic traces of material vision	snag ba'i bag chags
karmic traces of mental functioning	yid kyi bag chags
karmic traces of the material body	lus kyi bag chags
knowledge of things as they are	ji bzhin mkhyen pa
instantaneous awareness	skad cig shes pa
liberated into its own condition	rang sar grol
lucid	sal le ba
mind, mental functioning	yid (*manas*)
naked	rjen ne ba
natural, original, authentic	gnyug ma
natural clear light	rang bzhin 'od gsal
natural state	rnal ma
nature, inherent condition	rang bzhin
nature of mind	sems nyid

mindfulness, presence	dran pa
natural situation	gnas lugs
obscurations due to the passions	nyon mongs gyi sgrib pa
obscurations to knowledge	shes bya'i sgrib pa
period of contemplation	mnyam bzhag
passion	nyon mongs (*kleśa*)
potency	rtsal
potency of pure presence	rig pa'i rtsal
present	hrig ge ba
present in its own condition	rang sar gnas
primal awareness	ye shes
primal awareness of pure presence	rig pa'i ye shes
primal awareness of quantity	ji snyed ye shes
Primordial Yoga	gdod ma'i rnal 'byor (*Atiyoga*)
primordially occuring	ye babs
proceed along the path, to make (*something*) the path	lam khyer
progress in the practice	bogs dbyung
pure presence	rig pa
quietly	ting nger, lhan nger, tshan ner
real condition of existence	chos nyid (*dharmatā*)
to relax	glod pa, lhad pa
relax with presence	lhug pa
to recognize	ngo shes pa
self-liberation	rang grol
self-liberated as it arises	shar grol
self-liberated through bare attention	gcer grol
self-originated pure awareness	rang byung rig pa
settle into the natural state	rnal mar bzhag pa
sphere, bead	thig le (*bindu*)
stabilize, stable	brtan pa
surprised astonishment	had de ba
the state of, condition	ngang
state of being an ornament	rgyan gyi ngang
state of integration	mnyam nyid ngang
subject and object	gzung 'dzin
undistracted	yengs med
uncorrected, unmodified	ma bcos pa
understanding, to understand	rtogs pa
unmoving (*from the primordial state*)	g.yo med
vibrant	seng nge ba
whole dimension of one's life	'khor yug chen po
willingness to participate	dad pa

Tibetan-English

ka dag	primordially pure
skad cig shes pa	instantaneous awareness
sku *(kāya)*	dimension of existence
'khor yug chen po	the whole dimension of one's life
'khrul bral	free of illusions
glod pa	to relax
dgongs pa	intention, state
sgom nyams	experience during meditation
rgyan gyi ngnag	state of being an ornament
ngang	the state of, condition
ngo bo	essence
ngo shes pa	to recognize
gcer grol	self-liberated through bare attention
chos nyid *(dharmatā)*	real condition of existence
ting nge 'dzin *(samādhi)*	contemplation
ting nger	quietly
rtogs	understanding, to understand
brtan pa	stabilize, stable
thig le *(bindu)*	sphere, bead
thugs rje	Energy, compassion
ji snyed ye shes	primal awareness of quantity
ji bzhin mkhyen pa	knowledge of things as they are
rjen ne ba	naked
rjes nyams	experiences coming after meditation
rjes thob	after a period of contemplation
nyon mongs kyi sgrib pa	obscurations due to the passions
nyon mongs *(kleśa)*	passions
gnyug ma	natural, original, authentic
mnyam nyid ngnag	state of integration
mnyam bzhag	period of contemplation
dad pa	willingness to participate
de bzhin nyid	just as it is
dran pa	presence, mindfulness
gdod ma'i rnal 'byor	the Primordial Yoga, Atiyoga
bde ba'i nyams	experience of pleasurable sensation
nam mkha' ar gtad	integration into space
gnas lugs	natural situation
rnam rtog	discursive thought
rnal ma	natural state
rnal mar bzhag pa	to settle into the natural state
snang ba	appearance, to appear, to manifest, karmic vision
snang ba'i bag chags	karmic traces of material vision
dpyod pa	analysis, to analyze, examine
bag chags	karmic traces

bogs dbyung	to progress in practice
bying rgod	drowsiness and agitation
ma bcos	uncorrected, unmodified
mi rtog pa'i nyams	experience of non-discursiveness, emptiness
dmigs pa	conception, imagination
rtsal	potency
tshan ner	quietly
rdzogs chen	the Great Perfection
gzung 'dzin	subject and object
yid *(manas)*	mind, mental functioning
yid kyi bag chags	karmic traces of mental functioning
ye babs	primordially occurring
ye shes	primal awareness
yengs med	*undistracted*
g.yo med	unmoving (from the primordial state)
rang grol	self-liberation
rang byung rig pa	self-originated pure awareness
rang bzhin	nature, inherent nature
rang bzhin 'od gsal	natural clear light
rang sar gnas	to be present in its own condition
rang sar grol	liberated into its own condition
rig pa	pure presence, intrinsic awareness
rig pa'i rtsal	potency of pure presence
rig pa'i ye shes	primal awareness of pure presence
lam khyer	proceed along the path, make *(something)* the path
las kyi bag chags	karmic traces of the material body
shar grol	self-liberated as it arises
shes rgyun	continuity of awareness
shes pa	awareness, to know
shes bya'i sgrib pa	obscurations to knowledge
shes rab	intelligence
sal le ba	lucid
seng nge ba	vibrant
sems nyid	the nature of the mind
gsal bal	clarity, clear
gsal ba'i nyams	experience of clarity
bsam gran *(dhyāna)*	concentration
bsre ba	integrate, mix
had de ba	surprised astonishment
hrig ge ba	present
lhan ner	quietly
lhug pa	relaxed with presence, alertly relaxed
lhun grub	spontaneously self-perfected

The Cycle
of
Day and Night

(in Tibetan)

༄༅། །བོད་སྐད་དུ།

།གདོད་མའི་རྣལ་འབྱོར་གྱི་ལམ་ཁྱེར་

ཉིན་མཚན་འཁོར་ལོ་མ་ཞེས་བྱ་བ།

།བླ་མ་དམ་པ་རྣམས་ལ་ཕྱག་འཚལ་ལོ།

1 །རིགས་ཀུན་ཁྱབ་བདག་བྱང་ཆུབ་རྡོ་རྗེ་དང་།
།ཨོ་རྒྱན་བསྟན་འཛིན་རྡོ་རྗེ་དཔལ་སྒྲོན་སོགས།
།རྫོགས་ཆེན་བརྒྱུད་པའི་བླ་མ་ཐམས་ཅད་ལ།
།སྒོ་གསུམ་གུས་པ་ཆེན་པོས་ཕྱག་བགྱིའོ།

2 །ཀུན་བཟང་དཔལ་ལྡན་རྡོ་རྗེ་སེམས་དཔའ་ཡིས།
།ཨ་ཏི་ཡོ་གའི་སྙིང་པོ་ལམ་ཁྱེར་རྩལ།
།སྟོན་མཆོག་དགའ་རབ་རྡོ་རྗེར་གདམས་པའི་བཅུད།
།ཆུང་ཟད་སྤྲོ་ལ་མཁའ་འགྲོས་གནང་བར་མཛོད།

3 །རྟག་ཏུ་བློ་ལྡོག་རྣམ་བཞིས་རྒྱུད་སྦྱང་ཞིང་།
།རང་རིག་བླ་མར་ཤེས་པའི་རྣལ་འབྱོར་དང་།
།ནམ་ཡང་མི་འབྲལ་དུས་བཞིར་ཡེངས་མེད་དུ།
།དྲན་ཤེས་སྐྱོང་བ་རྣལ་འབྱོར་རྩ་བ་ཡིན།
4 །རྒྱུན་གྱི་འཁོར་ལོར་ཉིན་ཞག་ཐུ་གྣ་གཅིག་གི།
།ལམ་ཁྱེར་གཙོ་བོར་ཉིན་དང་མཚན་དུ་ངེས།
།དུས་གསུམ་དབང་ཕྱེད་ཉིན་མོའི་རྣལ་འབྱོར་ནི།
།རྟོགས་དང་བརྟན་དང་བོགས་དབྱུང་གསུམ་དུ་འདུ།
5 །ཐོག་མར་མ་རྟོགས་རྟོགས་པར་བྱ་བ་ནི།
།ཇི་སྙེད་སྣང་ཞིང་གྲགས་པའི་ཆོས་རྣམས་ཀུན།
།སྣ་ཚོགས་སྣང་ཡང་བདེན་མེད་གཟུགས་བརྙན་བཞིན།
།སེམས་ཀྱི་ཆོ་འཕྲུལ་ཉིད་དུ་ཁོ་ཐག་ཆོད།
6 །སེམས་ཉིད་ཡེ་ནས་སྟོང་ཞིང་བདག་མེད་ལ།
།མེད་བཞིན་གསལ་ལ་ཆ་འགགས་མེད་ཆུ་ཟླ་ལྟར།
།གསལ་སྟོང་གཉིས་མེད་རིག་པའི་ཡེ་ཤེས་མཆོག
།རང་བཞིན་ལྷུན་གྲུབ་ཉིད་དུ་རྟོགས་པར་བྱ།

7 །སྣང་བ་ཆོས་ཉིད་རྒྱན་དུ་ངོས་ཟིན་པས།
།ཚོགས་དྲུག་ལྷུག་པའི་སྣང་བ་རང་སར་གྲོལ།
།རིག་པ་ཡེ་ཤེས་ཉིད་དུ་ངོས་ཟིན་པས།
།ཉོན་མོངས་བག་ཆགས་སྣང་བ་རང་སར་གྲོལ།
8 །སྣང་རིག་དབྱེར་མེད་ཉིད་དུ་ངོས་ཟིན་པས།
།གཉིས་སུ་འཛིན་པའི་རྟོག་པ་རང་སར་གྲོལ།
།དེ་ཡང་གཅེར་གྲོལ་ཤར་གྲོལ་རང་གྲོལ་ཚུལ།
།རྣལ་འབྱོར་བློ་དང་བསྟུན་ཏེ་ལམ་དུ་ཁྱེར།
9 །ཐོལ་བྱུང་སྐད་ཅིག་དང་པོའི་ཤེས་པ་ནི།
།མ་བཅོས་སྐྱོ་མེད་ཤར་བའི་རིག་པ་སྟེ།
།གཟུང་འཛིན་མཐའ་ལས་འདས་པའི་དེ་བཞིན་ཉིད།
།གཉུག་མ་རང་བྱུང་རིག་པའི་ཡེ་ཤེས་ཡིན།
10 །དེ་ལ་ཀུན་བཟང་དགོངས་པའི་ཆོས་གསུམ་རྫོགས།
།བག་ཆགས་བྲལ་ཕྱིར་ཆོས་སྐུ་ངོ་བོ་སྟོང་།
།དམིགས་བསམ་བྲལ་ཕྱིར་ལོངས་སྐུ་རང་བཞིན་གསལ།
།ཞེན་ཆགས་བྲལ་བས་སྤྲུལ་སྐུ་འགགས་པ་མེད།

11 །དེ་ལྟར་ཤེས་པ་སྐྱེས་ཙམ་དེ་ཉིད་དུ།
།གཟུང་དང་འཛིན་པའི་གཉིས་རྟོག་ཡོངས་གྲོལ་ཞིང་།
།འཛིན་མེད་སྣང་བ་སྒྱི་ཟུ་གསལ་འཆར་ཏེ།
།སྣང་བ་ཆོས་ཉིད་ངང་དུ་གནས་པའོ།

12 །སྐད་ཅིག་མ་ཡི་ཤེས་པ་རྣལ་མ་ནི།
།ཆོས་ཉིད་མ་དང་འཕྲད་པས་ཆོས་ཀྱི་སྐུ།
།རིག་པ་ལྷུན་གྲུབ་ངང་ལ་གནས་པ་སྟེ།
།རྫོགས་པ་ཆེན་པོའི་དགོངས་པ་རྣལ་མ་ཡིན།

13 །བརྟན་པར་བསྐྱེ་དང་ལྷུག་པ་བོགས་དབྱུང་གི
།མན་ངག་གསུམ་གྱིས་ལམ་དུ་འཁྱེར་བ་སྟེ།
།བསྐྱེ་ཐབས་བདེ་བའི་སྟན་ལ་བག་ཡངས་སུ།
།ཁོང་གློད་མདུན་གྱི་མཁའ་ཀླུ་ཡར་ལ་གཏད།

14 །ཡེངས་མེད་སྒོམ་མེད་ལྷུག་པར་བཞག་པ་ན།
།ཤེས་པའང་མ་ཡའ་ལྷུར་འཛིན་ཞགས་གྲོལ་བའི་ངང་།
།གསལ་ཙམ་རིག་ཙམ་ཧད་དེར་གནས་དང་ཁྱུ།
།ཐ་དད་གཉིས་མེད་རིག་པ་རྗེན་གཅེར་ཤར།

15 །མཉམ་བཞག་བྱིང་རྒོད་དབང་དུ་མི་འགྲོ་བར།
།སལ་ལེ་ཧྲིག་གེ་ངང་ངེར་གནས་པའི་ངང་།
།དེ་ལ་དགུག་སྣང་བརྟན་སྤྲོས་ཅི་ཤར་ཀྱང་།
།གཡོ་མེད་རང་སར་གནས་ཤིང་རང་གྲོལ་ལ།

16 །རྗེས་ཐོབ་ཏིང་འཛིན་དེ་ལས་ལྡང་ན་ཡང་།
།ཤེས་པ་རྐྱེན་དབང་མི་འཚོར་བརྟན་པའི་ཚད།
།སྒོམ་ཉམས་འོད་དམ་ཉི་ཟླ་འཆར་འདྲ་དང་།
།སྣང་བ་དབུགས་སོགས་དམིགས་སུ་མེད་པ་འབྱུང་།

17 །རྗེས་ཉམས་ཀུན་སྣང་སྒྱུ་མར་མཐོང་བ་དང་།
།ཡང་ན་གང་སྣང་སྟོང་པར་འདུག་སྙམ་དང་།
།རིག་པ་མི་རྟོག་པ་ཟུ་ཚོར་བ་འམ།
།སྤྲོད་པར་གོལ་བ་མེད་པར་འདུག་སྙམ་འབྱུང་།

18 །སྐུ་ནི་ཡུལ་དཔྱོད་སེམས་རྟོག་སྟོང་མཐོང་ཕྱིར།
།སེམས་ཉིད་ཆོས་ཀྱི་སྐུ་མཆོག་ཐོབ་པ་དང་།
།ཡེ་ཤེས་མཚན་རྟོག་གང་གིས་མ་བསླད་པས།
།རྣམ་པར་མི་རྟོག་ཡེ་ཤེས་ཐོབ་པར་འགྱུར།

19 །བག་ཆགས་སྨིན་པ་ཡོངས་སུ་དག་པ་ཡིས།
།ཉོན་མོངས་མངོན་དུ་མི་སྐྱེ་བག་ལ་ཉལ།
།དེ་ཕྱིར་གང་ཟག་ཡིན་ཀྱང་འཁོར་གནས་ལས།
།གོང་དུ་འཕགས་པས་འཕགས་པའི་རིགས་སུ་ཤེས།

20 །ལྷུག་པའི་མན་ངག་ཕྱིར་སྣང་མ་བཅོས་པར།
།ཇི་ལྟར་ཤར་བ་རྒྱན་གྱི་ངང་ཉིད་དེར།
།ནང་རིག་མ་བཅོས་གསལ་སྟོང་རྗེན་ནེ་བ།
།དེ་བཞིན་ཉིད་དུ་རང་སར་གློད་དེ་ལྷུག

21 །ཚོགས་དྲུག་ཡུལ་ལ་མི་དཔྱོད་སལ་ལེ་བ།
།འགགས་མེད་རྒྱུན་དུ་ཤར་བ་དེ་བོ་ན།
།འཛིན་མེད་རིག་པའི་རྩལ་དུ་ཡོངས་རྫོགས་པས།
།གཉིས་མེད་ངང་དུ་སྐྱོང་བ་ལྷུག་པ་ཡིན།

22 །མཉམ་བཞག་སྒོ་ལྔའི་ཡུལ་ལ་མི་དཔྱོད་པར།
།གསལ་དྭངས་མི་གཡོ་འཛིན་མེད་ལྷུག་པར་ཤར།
།རྗེས་ཐོབ་གཟུགས་སྣང་མེད་བཞིན་སྣང་བ་སོགས།
།ཚོགས་དྲུག་ཡུལ་ལ་བརྟེན་པའི་ཡེ་ཤེས་སྐྱེ།

23 །ཉོན་མོངས་དུག་ལྔའི་ཀུན་རྟོག་གང་ཤར་བ།
།དེ་ཀའི་རང་ངོར་འཛིན་མེད་ལྷུག་པས་ཀྱང་།
།གཉེན་པོས་སྤང་དང་ཐབས་ཀྱིས་བསྒྱུར་མིན་པར།
།ཉོན་མོངས་ལམ་སློང་རང་གྲོལ་ཡེ་ཤེས་སྐྱེ།
24 །སྒོམ་ཉམས་གསལ་ཞིང་སྟོང་པར་སྣང་བ་དང་།
།སྣང་ལ་སྟོང་པའི་ངང་དུ་གནས་པ་དང་།
།འགྱུ་ཞིང་སྟོང་དང་བདེ་ལ་སྟོང་པ་སོགས།
།བདེ་གསལ་མི་རྟོག་ཤེས་ཉམས་ཅི་རིགས་འབྱུང་།
25 །སྐུ་ནི་ཆོས་ཀུན་ཆོས་ཀྱི་སྐུར་རྟོགས་ཏེ།
།མ་བཅོས་ཤེས་པ་དེ་བཞིན་ཉིད་ཀྱི་ངང་།
།གཉིས་མེད་མཉམ་རྫོགས་ཐིག་ལེར་བཟླུམ་པའི་ཕྱིར
།ཡེ་ཤེས་སྐུ་ཐོབ་གསལ་བའི་ཡེ་ཤེས་སྐྱེ།
26 །གཟུང་ཡུལ་ཆོས་ཉིད་སྣང་བས་ཉོན་སྒྲིབ་དག
།རིག་པའི་ཡེ་ཤེས་སྐྱེས་ཕྱིར་ཚུལ་ངན་གྲོལ།
།ཉོན་མོངས་བག་ཆགས་སྒྲིབ་ལས་རྣམ་གྲོལ་བས།
།འཕགས་པ་བྱང་ཆུབ་སེམས་དཔའི་རིགས་སུ་ཤེས།

27 །ཐོགས་དཀྲུང་མ་བཅོས་ལྷུན་གྲུབ་ངང་ཉིད་དེར།
།སྐད་ཅིག་ཤེས་པ་མ་བཅོས་ལྷན་ནེར་བཞག
།མི་རྟོག་རིག་པ་སལ་ལེ་ཧྲིག་གེ་བ།
།ཤེས་རྒྱུན་དེ་ཀ་མ་ཡེངས་བརྟན་པར་བསྐྱང་།

28 །མཉམ་བཞག་བྱིང་རྒོད་དབང་དུ་མི་འགྱུར་བར།
།ཆོས་ཉིད་སྟོང་པ་ཉིད་དུ་སྣང་བ་དང་།
།རྗེས་ཐོབ་ཤེས་པ་རྐྱེན་དབང་མི་འགྱུར་བར།
།སེམས་ཉིད་དེ་བཞིན་ཉིད་དུ་བསྐྱང་བར་བྱ།

29 །སྒོམ་ཉམས་བསྒོམ་དང་མི་བསྒོམ་གཉིས་མེད་དང་།
།ཀུན་སྣང་ཏིང་འཛིན་རོལ་པར་ཡོངས་ཤར་ཞིང་།
།ཆོས་རྣམས་ཀུན་གྱི་ཆོས་ཉིད་ཇི་བཞིན་པ།
།ཡེ་བབ་གནས་ལུགས་ངང་ལས་གཡོ་མེད་འབྱུང་།

30 །སྐུ་ནི་སྣང་དང་མི་སྣང་ཆོས་རྣམས་ཀུན།
།ཆོས་ཉིད་ངང་དུ་རང་སར་ཡོངས་དག་པས།
།གཉིས་སུ་མེད་པའི་སྐུ་མཆོག་ཐོབ་པ་དང་།
།གོས་པ་མེད་པའི་ཡེ་ཤེས་དམ་པ་སྐྱེ།

31 །ཤེས་བྱའི་སྒྲིབ་པ་རྣམ་པར་དག་པའི་ཕྱིར།
།ཆོས་ཀུན་ཆོས་ཉིད་ཇི་བཞིན་མཁྱེན་པ་དང་།
།རྟོགས་བྱ་རྟོགས་བྱེད་གཉིས་མེད་ཡོངས་གྲོལ་བས།
།རྣམ་མཁྱེན་དེ་བཞིན་གཤེགས་པའི་རིགས་སུ་ཤེས།

32 །མཚན་མོའི་རྣལ་འབྱོར་ལམ་དུ་ཁྱེར་བ་ནི།
།སྲོད་དང་ཐོ་རངས་རྣལ་འབྱོར་གཉིས་ལ་བསླབ།
།སྲོད་ལ་དབང་པོ་མཉམ་པར་བཞག་པ་སྟེ།
།དེ་ཡང་བསམ་གཏན་གཉིད་དང་བསྲེ་བར་བྱ།
33 །གཉིད་དུ་ལོག་ཁར་རང་གི་སྙིང་མཚམས་སུ།
།ཨ་ཡིག་དཀར་པོའམ་འོད་ལྔའི་ཐིག་ལེ་ནི།
།སྲན་མའི་གོང་བུ་ཙམ་དུ་གསལ་བ་ལ།
།ཤེས་པ་གཏད་ཅིང་ལྷོད་དེ་གཉིད་དུ་ལོག
34 །ཀུན་ཏུ་རྟོག་པའི་དྲི་མས་མ་སྦགས་ཤིང་།
།ཚོགས་དྲུག་རང་སར་ལྷུག་པའི་ངང་ཉིད་དུ།
།གཉིད་དུ་ཕེབས་ན་རང་བཞིན་འོད་གསལ་ཏེ།

།མི་རྟོག་ཆོས་ཉིད་ངང་དུ་གནས་པར་འགྱུར།
35 །ཡང་ན་སྐད་ཅིག་ཤེས་པ་ལ་བལྟས་པས།
།གནས་འགྱུའི་རང་ངོ་གང་ཡང་མཐོང་མེད་པ།
།སེང་ངེ་བ་ཞིག་འབྱུང་བ་དེ་ཀའི་ངང་།
།ཤེས་པ་ཙན་ནེར་བཞག་ཅིང་གཉིད་དུ་ལོག
36 །གཉིད་དེས་ཆོས་ཉིད་གསལ་བའི་རྐྱེན་བྱས་ནས།
།རིག་པ་ཆོས་དབྱིངས་ངང་ལ་ཡོངས་གྲིམ་སྐྱེ།
།ཇི་སྲིད་གཉིད་དུ་ལོག་པའི་རྐྱེན་དེ་སྲིད།
།ཆོས་ཉིད་ཁོ་ནའི་ངང་དུ་གནས་པ་འགྱུར།
37 །ལུས་ཀྱི་བག་ཆགས་སྣང་བའི་བག་ཆགས་དང་།
།ཡིད་ཀྱི་བག་ཆགས་རྣམས་དང་ཡོངས་བྲལ་ནས།
།ཡིད་མི་འབྱུང་ཞིང་ཆོས་ཉིད་ངང་གནས་པ།
།རང་བཞིན་འོད་གསལ་འཆར་བའི་ཚོད་དུ་ཤེས།
38 །གཉིད་ཀྱི་རྟོག་པ་གང་ཡང་མི་འབྱུང་ཞིང་།
།རིག་པ་མར་གྲིམ་ཆོས་ཉིད་ངང་དུ་གནས།
།རྗེས་ཐོབ་རྨི་ལམ་ཉིད་དུ་ངོ་ཤེས་ཤིང་།

།འཁྲུལ་གྲོལ་སྐུ་དང་ཡེ་ཤེས་གྲོགས་སུ་ཤར།
39 །གོ་རངས་ཡེ་ཤེས་རང་སོ་མ་བཅོས་པ།
།སྒོམ་མེད་ཡེངས་མེད་རྣལ་མར་བཞག་པ་ན།
།རང་བཞིན་མི་རྟོག་ལྷན་ནེར་གནས་པ་དེ།
།བླ་མ་ཀུན་ཏུ་བཟང་པོའི་དགོངས་པར་ཤེས།
40 །དེ་ཀའི་རང་ངོར་བལྟས་ཏེ་སྒོམ་མཁན་ལ།
།གཅེར་གྱིས་བལྟས་པས་ངོས་བཟུང་བྲལ་བ་ཡི།
།རང་བྱུང་ཡེ་ཤེས་སལ་ལེ་རྗེན་ནེ་བ།
།ཤར་གྲོལ་གཉིས་མེད་ཡེ་ཤེས་སྐྱེ་བར་འགྱུར།
41 །དེ་ཚེ་གཉིས་འཛིན་ཀུན་རྟོག་ལས་འདས་པའི།
།སྣང་བ་ཡུལ་གྲོལ་མི་རྟོག་ཡེ་ཤེས་གསལ།
།ཤེས་པས་མ་བསླད་གསལ་བའི་ཡེ་ཤེས་གསལ།
།གཉིས་སུ་མེད་པས་བདེ་བའི་ཡེ་ཤེས་གསལ།
42 །ཆོས་ཀུན་ཆོས་ཉིད་རང་དུ་རྟོགས་འགྱུར་བས།
།གོལ་བ་མེད་པའི་ཡེ་ཤེས་མཆོག་ཏུ་གསལ།
།རྗེ་སྟོང་ཡེ་ཤེས་ཡོངས་སུ་གསལ་བ་ཡིས།

།སྐུ་གསུམ་རང་བཞིན་མཆོག་ཏུ་གསལ་བར་འགྱུར།

43 །དེ་ལྟར་རྣལ་འབྱོར་སྙིང་པོ་ཉིན་མཚན་དུ།

།ཏིང་འཛིན་ཁོར་ཡུག་ཆེན་པོར་བསྒྲིམས་པ་ན།

།འབྱོངས་དང་ཉོན་མོངས་ལམ་སློང་སྐུ་གསུམ་གྱིས།

།མཁའ་མཉམ་འགྲོ་དོན་བྱེད་པའི་ཚད་ངེས་འགྱུར།

44 །འབྱོངས་ཚད་ཀྱི་ལམ་ཉིད་དུ་ངོ་ཤེས་ཤིང་།

།བདེ་སྟོང་ཞེན་པས་མ་གོས་མཉམ་ཉིད་ངང་།

།ཡེ་ཤེས་སྒྱུ་འཕྲུལ་ཀུན་སྣང་གྲོགས་སུ་ཤར།

།འཁྲུལ་པའི་རྒྱུན་ཆད་ཆོས་ཉིད་ངང་ལ་གནས།

45 །ཨ་ཧོ་ཡོ་གའི་ཉམས་ལེན་པ་དེ་ནི།

།ཉིན་མཚན་ཆོས་ཉིད་ངང་ལས་མ་གཡོས་ཕྱིར།

།དབུགས་ཀྱི་བར་མ་དོནས་འཚང་རྒྱ་ཞེས།

།བདག་ཉིད་ཆེན་པོ་དགའ་རབ་རྡོ་རྗེས་གསུངས།

46 །ཉོན་མོངས་ལམ་སློང་ཆོས་ཀུན་དབྱེར་མེད་པར།

།ཆོས་ཉིད་ངང་གནས་ཀུན་རིག་དམིགས་མེད་ཕྱིར།

།གཏི་མུག་མི་རྟོག་པ་རུ་ངོ་ཤེས་པས།

།ཆོས་ཉིད་དེ་བཞིན་ཉིད་དུ་སྣང་བ་ཡིན།
47 །ཚོགས་དྲུག་ཡུལ་དུ་སྣང་བའི་ཆོས་རྣམས་ཀུན།
།གསལ་ལ་རང་བཞིན་མེད་པར་གནས་པའི་ཕྱིར།
།ཞི་སྣང་གསལ་བའི་རང་བཞིན་ངོ་ཤེས་པས།
།གསལ་བ་ཡེ་ཤེས་ཉིད་དུ་སྣང་བ་ཡིན།
48 །ཕྱིར་སྣང་ཆོས་ཉིད་ནང་རིག་ཡེ་ཤེས་ཏེ།
།གཉིས་མེད་བདེ་ཆེན་ཐུགས་རྗེའི་བདག་ཉིད་ཕྱིར།
།འདོད་ཆགས་བདེ་ཆེན་རྩལ་དུ་ངོ་ཤེས་པས།
།ལྷུན་འཁྲུམས་བདེ་ཆེན་ཡེ་ཤེས་སྣང་བ་ཡིན།
49 །སྐུ་གསུམ་སྒོ་ནས་འགྲོ་དོན་འབྱུང་བ་ཡང་།
།ཉོན་མོངས་དུག་གསུམ་སྐུ་དང་ཡེ་ཤེས་སུ།
།ཡོངས་སུ་སྣང་ཕྱིར་དེ་ལས་བྱུང་བ་ཀུན།
།སྐུ་དང་ཡེ་ཤེས་ཉིད་དུ་གནས་པ་ཡིན།
50 །ཉོན་མོངས་མེད་པས་འཁོར་བའི་རྒྱུ་བྲལ་བ།
།དེ་ལ་རྒྱུད་འདས་ཞེས་སུ་བརྗོད་མོད་ཀྱང་།
།མ་བཅོས་ལྷུན་གྲུབ་བ་ཏེ་སྐྱིད་ཡོན་ཏན་ཚོགས།

།ཉིན་ཕྱེད་མཁའ་ལ་འཆར་བ་ཞིན་གསལ་བ་ཙམ།
51 །ཚུལ་འདི་དད་བརྩོན་ཅན་པ་ཉིང་འཛིན་དང་།
།ཤེས་རབ་དབང་ལྡན་གདུལ་བྱའི་སྤྱོད་ཡུལ་དུ།
།ཐེག་པ་མཆོག་ལས་ཇི་ལྟར་གདམས་པ་བཞིན།
།མཐུན་ཆེན་རྫོགས་པར་བསྒྲུབ་ལ་མཁས་པར་ཤོག།
52 །དེ་སྐད་ཀུན་བཟང་དགའ་རབ་རྡོ་རྗེ་ཡི།
།དགོངས་བརྒྱུད་ཀུང་དུའི་ཚིག་ཏུ་དྲིལ་བའི་དགེས།
།བདག་ཅག་མཁའ་མཉམ་འགྲོ་བ་ཐོབ་མ་ལུས་པ།
།ཀུན་བཟང་རྒྱལ་བའི་གོ་འཕང་མྱུར་ཐོབ་ཤོག

འདི་ནི་ཐེག་པ་མཆོག་གི་ཉལ་
འབྱོར་ལ་མོས་པ་ཨ་མཆོག་ལྡན་སྐྱུ་ཞབས་
པཱུལ་ཨ་ནྡེར་སོན་སྐུ་ཞི་བར་གཤེགས་
པའི་དྲན་གསོས་སུ་ཆེད་དུ་དམིགས་
ཏེ། ཨ་རིའི་ཤར་ཕྱོགས་ཀྱི་ལྗོངས་སུ་
ཡོད་པའི་ཁོན་ཕྱེ་རྫོགས་ཆེན་འདུས་

སྔར་ནི་མཚམས་དབུ་ཚུགས་པའི་ཚེ

ཆེན་དུ་དམིགས་ཏེ། རྫོགས་ཆེན་པ་

ནམ་མཁའི་ནོར་བུས་ཆུ་མོ་ཕག་གི་ལོ་

ཧོར་ཟླ་བརྒྱད་པའི་ཚེས་སུམ་ཅུ་བཀྲ་ཤིས་

ཉི་མའི་ཉིན་རྫོགས་པར་སྦྱོལ་བ་དགེ།།